The Second Torpedo

Other books by Ilene Birkwood

Fiction

Suddenly Silence

Deadly Deception

Nonfiction

Stress for Success

The Second Torpedo

Ilene Birkwood

ISBN: 1-4810-1908-2
ISBN-13: 9781481019088

To Darren and Duncan

Grandsons Extraordinaire

Acknowledgments

I wish to thank John Roberts, a fellow survivor, for information that has been vital in writing this book. Indeed, if it had not been for John taking the time to track me down, this book would never have been written. My thanks too to Alan Corbishley who has been extremely helpful and has provided both information and photos.

Many thanks to George Malcolmson, Archivist at the Royal Naval Submarine Museum in Gosport for his patience, helpfulness, and the excellent information regarding the U-boat and Adalbert Schnee.

Thanks also to Graham Bennett, Curator of the Ventnor Local History Society, and to Fay Brown for the information on the Ventnor Radar Station raids.

To the Isle of Wight County Press, and in particular Anna Jones, many thanks for your help in providing newspaper articles regarding the incident.

Thanks to Janet Sinclair, An Iodhlann's archivist on the delightful island of Tiree in Scotland's outer isles, for the information regarding the purser.

Thanks also to my traveling companion on the *Volendam* Jill Mason (nee Brown), who provided information, photos, and many shared laughs over our six- and seven-year-old selves.

My profound appreciation is extended to all the survivors who took the time to share their experiences with me. Among the survivors, copious information has been circulating for years. I have received much of this second or third hand. So although I do not know your names, I am indebted to you all. If there is anyone I have omitted to mention or give credit to, please contact me, and I will rectify this in future editions.

My thanks to the Quixotics: Meg Hellyer, Frances Evlin, Trish Corbett, Jeanette Keil, and Mac McCullough, whose astute comments and constant encouragement made writing this book such an enjoyable experience.

My heartfelt gratitude to the crew of the *Volendam*. Their efficiency saved our lives, and their unfailing good humor made the whole shipwreck an exciting childhood adventure.

Introduction

To discover late in life that you should have gone to a watery grave before your eighth birthday is a strange experience.

It began like this . . .

On one of our annual visits to England, my husband and I watched from the balcony of our condominium as a ketch navigated the lock in Brighton Marina. Fascinated, we saw it rise to meet the incoming tide. In the marina below us, the yachts' rigging jingled in the breeze that whipped the sea beyond the seawall into an uneven chop.

When the phone rang, I checked the caller ID. Puzzled, I wondered what salesman was working this late on a Friday evening.

"Hello, this is John Roberts. Are you Ilene Birkwood?" The voice cultured and charming.

"Yes." I still suspected a sales ploy.

"You won't remember me, but I traveled with you on the *Volendam* in 1940."

"Really?" My interest quickened. I hadn't met anyone from the *Volendam* in decades. I moved indoors. The breeze, seagulls, and rigging made listening difficult.

"Could we get together? I've some information for you. I'd be curious to know if you remember any more than I do."

"I doubt it. I remember being seasick in the lifeboat though."

"Me too!" We both laughed.

He continued to talk and as I listened, telephone cradled between shoulder and ear, my mind wandered. I felt again the spines of the lifeboat sticking in my back and the spray from the black mountainous waves in my face. I was brought abruptly back to the present as he asked for directions to the marina.

After he said good-bye, I put down the phone and sat looking at it for several minutes. My husband came in from the balcony, looked at my face, and said, "What's the matter?"

"Oh, nothing," I said nonchalantly. "Just an old friend. I've invited him over on Sunday."

"That's good, but what did he say?"

"He told me about something that happened on the *Volendam*."

Note: This book is a combination of personal memories, recollections gleaned from conversations with other survivors, and research material supplied by fellow travelers and ever-helpful archivists.

Chapter One

In WWII, Hitler's armies swept across Europe and faced by a simultaneous attack from well-trained troops and the Luftwaffe, the unprepared countries fell. Poland, Denmark, Norway, Holland, and Belgium were defeated and Sweden and Switzerland declared neutrality. Finally, when France capitulated in May 1940, Britain stood alone. The German army massed in Northern France and Belgium ready to invade Britain.

When France fell, a French general famously said, "If Britain decides to fight on, she will be wrung by her neck like a chicken in three weeks."

They had discounted Churchill, who responded with, "But what a chicken, and what a neck!"

He then gave his inspirational speech: "We shall defend our island whatever the cost may be, we shall fight on the beaches, we shall fight on the landing grounds, we shall fight in the fields and in the streets, we shall fight in the hills. We shall never surrender." The country, promised only "blood, toil, tears, and sweat," buckled down for a long, hard fight.

As the Nazi forces advanced, the horrified world watched pictures of women and children being killed, maimed, and rendered homeless by Hitler's blitzkrieg. With innocent citizens in the same danger as frontline troops, peoples' thoughts turned to the children. Throughout the Dominions and the United States, women's organizations developed schemes to evacuate children from the "front line" to the safety of homes in their countries.

In September 1939, Canada's National Council of Women organized a national register of women for war work, and one hundred thousand women offered their homes to evacuees. In addition, committee members contacted friends at the universities of Birmingham, Manchester, Oxford, and Cambridge and the day France capitulated, invited them to send their staff's children to Toronto. The faculty at Toronto provided homes and financial help to the children. Harvard and Yale faculties extended the same hospitality. Similarly, corporations made offers to their British branches. For example, the president of Ford of Canada sponsored 102 children of Ford's British employees.

In May 1940, an official invitation was extended to British children by the four Dominions of Canada, Australia, New Zealand and South Africa. Britain, overwhelmed by formal and informal offers of refuge for children, formed the Children's Overseas Reception Board (CORB).

Across the Dominions, thousands offered their homes. Reasons for the offer differed, but many did it out of a sense of patriotism. They felt they were thwarting Hitler by whisking children out of harm's way.

The ties between Britain and the Dominions were strong, and when Britain faced invasion, young men from the Dominions volunteered in the thousands to stand shoulder-to-shoulder with their British counterparts. Their womenfolk felt equally committed and volunteered to look after evacuees as their part of the war effort.

U.S. women were no less generous in their offers, but no formal government invitation was extended. The American Committee for the Evacuation of Children operated through the U.S. Consul in London.

The British Government appointed Geoffrey Shakespeare, Under-Secretary of State for the Dominions, as chairman of CORB. He put together a committee that he maintained accomplished more in three weeks than most parliamentary committees do in months. With invasion imminent, speed was essential, and committee members worked as many as ninety hours per week.

Within six weeks of the invitation from the Dominions being received, the first children sailed from Liverpool. As Geoffrey Shakespeare said, "It is surely inspiring that lovers of freedom, far removed from the war zone, are so concerned about the safety of our children."

Evacuation was offered to children living in vulnerable areas, and the South Coast of England, in some areas a scant twenty miles from France, was particularly vulnerable.

*   *   *

I pushed the shrimping net deep beneath the overhanging rocks of the tide pool and caught five fat shrimps, long and opaque, with their tails turned in. I emptied them into my Flash Gordon pail. Small crabs scurried away as I moved farther along the pool, following the receding tide. If I shrimped as the tide ebbed, I could fill my pail in record time. I waded deeper and deeper into the pool, totally focused on my net, heedless of saturated shorts.

"Have you caught many?" The man's voice made me jump. I looked up to see a man and woman picking their way barefoot across the slippery seaweed on the rocks above the pool. Behind them, the sky was a cloudless blue. Wordless, I held out my pail for him to see.

The woman, with pretty blonde hair and twinkling eyes, said, "Gosh, you have done well, but shouldn't you be going home? It's getting late."

Startled, I looked around and noticed the beach was almost empty. My friends still sat on the sand, inspecting their catch, but after a long hot day, everyone else had gathered up their towels and deck chairs and headed home for dinner. As I started to scramble up on the rocks, she held out a soft, warm hand. Taking it, I continued to stare at her speechless.

"I think your mother is going to be pleased to see the shrimp, but not those wet shorts," she added with a smile.

For the first time I noticed the soggy shorts that clung wetly to my skinny legs. I was not worried. My mother was used to clothes continually muddy, grass-stained or stiff with salt water and she seldom scolded me. I was the spoiled youngest child of four and totally disinterested in pretty clothes or dolls. I preferred climbing cliffs or playing Robin Hood with bows and arrows.

With straight brown hair parted on one side and roasted a gentle brown by the sun, I smiled shyly, eyes downcast, and said, "Thank you very much. I had better go home now." I scurried off to join my friends. Behind me, I heard the man and woman laughing as they watched my sloshing progress through the long pool.

My friends jumped to their feet when they saw me coming, and together, we walked up the slipway that led to the road. My black Labrador, Bruce, joined me, nuzzling my hand with his gray muzzle. Together, we skipped and plodded home, leaving a trail of seawater behind us.

The smell of Cornish pasties and apple pie greeted me as I rushed in through the kitchen door. My mother praised my catch and told me to hurry up and get a bath before dinner. I shed my wet clothes and ran upstairs, knowing that Hazel—my eldest sister, who, at thirteen, was seven years older than me—would help run the bath.

When I was three, she taught me how to read and write. Each day she set up a "class" that I had to attend. She looked up from the attendance book and called my name. I jumped to my feet and said, "Present." She meticulously ticked off my name, the only pupil, in her book. When I started real nursery school at the age of four, I could already read and write.

We lived in a big house near a sandy beach on the western end of the Isle of Wight. The Island, as we all called it, is diamond-shaped, twenty miles from east to west and twelve miles from north to south. A picturesque spot with villages of thatched cottages and even a thatched church, it is a popular holiday destination with its many good beaches and spectacular walks across the downs. The downs, rolling chalk hills that stretch the length of the island and afford spectacular views, are swept by invigorating salt air. As Alfred Lord Tennyson, who lived there for many years, said, "The air is so good it should be bottled and sold for a shilling a pint."

Poets seem to favor the island—Keats and Byron spent time and waxed lyrical there, and Longfellow visited. He too wrote a poem, but since it was after a visit to a pub, it was not one of his better ones.

Tennyson wrote most of his famous poems in a beautiful home only about a couple of miles from where I lived. Years after he died, his estate was sold and my mother, who loved going to auctions, bought Tennyson's dining room table. It was huge and completely filled our dining room, but it made a great ping-pong table between meals.

Living in a quiet country area, I was free to roam with my friends and in the summer we spent all our time on the beach, rowing, fishing, and swimming. Sometimes, we were given a trip in the excursion motorboat to the mainland to visit Hurst Castle, where Charles I had been imprisoned. I loved the dungeons where the tide came in, swamping the poor prisoners.

Five days after my shrimping venture, on September 3, 1939, Britain declared war on Germany. Little changed, but we were expected to sit in complete silence every evening when the BBC came on the radio.

"Good evening, this is the BBC home service, the six o'clock news with Bruce Belfrage." Mr. Belfrage told us about the invasion of Poland and Britain's declaration of war.

All men fit for service between the ages of twenty and thirty-six were conscripted. Everyone else, men and women alike, had to do war work. My father—at fifty-four, well over conscription age—became a coastguard. Every night or morning (according to his shift), he donned a khaki uniform, strapped a rifle and helmet on his back, and cycled to the coastguard station about a mile and a half away. The station was at the end of a row of coastguard cottages on a bluff overlooking the Solent, the narrow strip of water that divides the Island from the mainland. Armed with a high-powered telescope, binoculars, searchlight, rifle, and Tommy gun, he sat watch for eight hours, scanning the sea for any German ship or U-boat creeping up the Solent.

I used to think the news at the movie house dull, but after the war started, it became exciting. Pictures of storm troopers in their shining high boots goose-stepping into capital after capital as Denmark, Norway, Holland, and Belgium fell. Pictures of airmen, looking not much older than my twelve-year old brother, dressed in heavy wool-lined leather flying jackets scrambling to their fighters as the Luftwaffe bombed their airfield. Land Army girls wearing big smiles, harvesting corn. Factory workers furiously turning out arms and ammunition. It was all action. Much better than dull politicians making speeches.

We hurried home after each movie in case the air raid siren sounded. In the pitch dark, with no street lights, flashlights or lights from any of the houses—a total blackout. Air raid wardens on bicycles rode around, shouting "Put that light out," to anyone who had a chink in their curtains.

We still played all day, but if the siren went while we were on the beach, we ran home to take shelter. Finally, in the summer of 1940, the beaches were closed. Together with three of my friends, I decided to go and see why. At the beach end of our road, men were setting up big cement blocks.

Robbie, the boldest of our gang, asked in a high piping voice, "What are those things for?"

A young workman stopped, mopped his sweaty brow with a crumpled blue handkerchief, and said, "They're to stop the Jerry tanks coming up the road." He gestured with his shovel. "And that barbed wire is going to be strung between them to stop the troops."

We all stared, outraged to think nasty Germans would come up *our* road. A gray-haired workman hurried over. "Jim, just you shut up and stop scaring the kids." Turning to us, he added, "And you run along home and play. We'll take care of those Jerrys." He brandished his spade towards the sea. Giggling, we ran up the road to my garden.

About a week later, Robbie found a way down to the beach over a low cliff. After they finished building the tank defenses, we sneaked down to play on the beach when no adults were around.

In May 1940, when the evening news told us that France had fallen, my father said, "This is it." I wondered what "it" was. Then, a couple of days later, the news ended with an announcement: "The British Expeditionary Force is hemmed in on the beach at Dunkirk. Would anyone with a pleasure craft over thirty feet volunteer to go over to France and help pick them up." Everyone with a boat large enough rushed to their aid. Pleasure boats from the yacht harbors of Cowes and Yarmouth went—luxury yachts, beat up old day sailers, fishing boats, and even the lifeboats. Everyone with a boat large enough answered the call. I was told later the Admiralty only expected thirty thousand troops to be saved, but seven hundred little vessels went over, and 338,226 British and French soldiers were saved. The "little ships" ferried troops standing shoulder-high in sea water to the naval ships standing offshore.

Mr. Churchill came on the radio one evening and said that the German army was getting ready to invade us. The Isle of Wight, only a few miles off the South Coast of England, close to France, was in a vulnerable position. It stood between France and the commercial port of Southampton—home to large luxury liners like the *Queen Mary*—and Portsmouth, Britain's premier naval base.

On a warm summer evening in late August, the sun streamed through the windows of our sitting room, and the breeze coming through the open window smelled faintly of dust from the brown-tinged lawn. Feeling sleepy after a big meal and a long day playing in the sun, I planned to go out in the garden and practice tennis by hitting a ball against the wall of the house. I made for the door, intent on getting there before I was bundled off to bed. Just as I put my hand on the shiny brass doorknob, my father said, "Come and sit down all of you. I have something to tell you."

Instantly wide awake because my father, a quiet man, seldom made announcements, I scurried to a big, overstuffed armchair and perched on the arm. I noticed my two sisters' and brother's faces alert with curiosity as they gathered around him. He tapped the tobacco down in his pipe, looked at it a moment before scraping a Swan Vestas match across the box, and puffed a few times until the flame ignited the tobacco. A blue haze floated up to the ceiling, and the comfortable smell of Robin Redbreast tobacco wafted across to me.

The room was still warm from the setting sun, and a bee buzzed angrily at the window pane, loud in the silence. Sitting in his favorite armchair, my father took a few puffs on his pipe, laid it down in an ashtray, and said, "You are going to Canada to stay with your auntie and uncle until the war is over."

We all beamed from ear to ear. My mother sat, eyes downcast, hands tightly clasped, and said nothing. None of us questioned the decision. In those far-off heady days, the parent's word was law.

My brother, stuttering slightly in his excitement, asked, "W-when will we be going?"

"I don't know yet. The Ministry told us you will be going soon and to get everything ready. We'll know soon enough, and then you'll be off." Looking serious, he added, "Now, this is to be a secret adventure. You're not to tell your friends or your schoolmates or any of the neighbors that you're going. I know it's going to be hard to keep a secret, but that's instructions from the Ministry." He picked up his pipe and waved it to emphasize the point, creating a faint blue/gray loop in the air. "They don't want you to give information to the Germans. Remember 'Careless Talk Costs Lives.'"

As if we could forget. The slogan was everywhere—at the movie theater, in the church hall, even at school.

Excitement bubbled up inside me. It sounded very much as if we were going on an outing. I had only been on one before. A Sunday school outing for the day to Sandown, twenty whole miles away. We had a wonderful time—games on the beach and lots of ice cream.

Even more exciting was the fact that we were all going together. As the youngest, I was sometimes left behind with my mother.

That night, excitement won over sleep for about half an hour, but a few hours later, I was sound asleep when the air raid siren wailed its strident notes, up and down, up and down. We ran downstairs in the dark. Every light in the house was out, and black out curtains covered the windows. We knew we must never show a light when the warning sounded. My mother made a joke of it by serving lots of carrots and telling us they would help us see in the dark.

Air raids happened quite often, even in the daytime. On a school day, we went to the shelters there. After the siren sounded, our teacher told us to pick up our gas masks and emergency rations and follow her in a crocodile to the shelter. My emergency rations were in a Mickey Mouse lunch pail. My mother packed a sandwich, an apple, a bottle of water and a roll of wine gums. She told me the wine gums were for emergencies only. I eyed them longingly during each raid, hoping the teacher would tell us it was an emergency.

We walked across the playground through a gate to a little lane that led to the Anderson shelters in a field behind the school. The shelters, sunk into the ground, had domed corrugated iron roofs, wooden benches lining each wall, and one down the middle. We sang songs and recited poems until the all-clear siren sounded one long note and finally died away.

At home, we simply ran downstairs to the kitchen. With a three-story brick-and-tile house, we felt safe on the ground floor. My father had a bucket of sand, one of water, and a stirrup pump in the kitchen and attic ready to fight any fires caused by incendiary bombs. The large kitchen had a door leading to the dining room, one to the pantry and another to a porch. My mother and father sat in chairs. We lay on mattresses, and my aunt, who was visiting after having survived an air raid on the mainland that destroyed her house, sat in a closet under the stairs—the safest place in the house—with a cushion on top of her head. We children thought it hilarious.

Councils were busy supplying each house with a shelter—a splendid brick and reinforced concrete affair for our garden. However, it took time to build these shelters, and my father, having fought in WWI, knew we needed shelter immediately. So he built a dugout—a large hole in the ground with a corrugated iron roof, and earth and sod piled on top. It was very efficient and would have kept us safe. Unfortunately, it kept filling with water. This inspired my eleven-year-old sister Margaret to write the following:

OUR SHELTER
Our shelter is a dugout,
All filled with water.
It needs a bailing out, it does.
To save us from the slaughter.

Sadly, she did not go on to become poet laureate.

Living in the country, we were not under direct attack, but German bombers chased by British fighters sometimes off-loaded their bombs to speed up their escape. I could hear the throb of the bombers and the screech of the fighters and the far-off sound of artillery batteries opening up. I heard my father saying quietly, "Sounds as if Southampton is copping it again."

Sleep overcame me until the long drawn-out wail of the all-clear siren died and my sister poked me in the ribs. Back to bed in the dark, and then up at first light to watch the dog fights overhead as the Spitfires pursued the Messerschmitts back across the channel.

The days crept by as my mother, aware that she would only receive two days warning of our departure date, painstakingly sewed labels in our clothes and purchased suitcases in accordance with the instructions sent to her by the Children's Overseas Reception Board (CORB):

Each child should be dressed in a coat with the large white
CORB label pinned on the front.
Children should carry a gas mask at all times.
Each child should have a suitcase packed with the attached list
of clothes (figure 1)
All clothes should be clearly marked in indelible ink.
NO trunks will be allowed
NO passports are needed.

The things needed for two nights (pajamas, toothbrush, and wash bag) should be packed in a separate haversack. Food sufficient for twelve hours should be carried together with thirst-quenching fruit or a carton of water or milk. The following are suggested and easy to pack:

Sandwiches, egg, and cheese
Packets of nuts and seedless raisins
Dry biscuits and packets of cheese
Barley sugar (not chocolate)
Apples

Figure 1 List of Clothes

GIRLS

Gas mask
1 warm coat and Macintosh if possible
1 cardigan or woollen jumper
1 hat or beret
1 pair warm gloves
1 warm dress or skirt and jumper
2 pairs stockings
1 change of underclothes including vests, knickers, etc.
1 pair strong boots or shoes
1 pair plimsolls
2 cotton dresses or overalls with knickers
2 pairs pajamas
1 towel
6 handkerchiefs
1 hairbrush and comb
1 toothbrush and paste
1 face flannel or sponge
1 linen bag
1 suitcase – about 26" x 18"
1 attache case or haversack
sewing outfit
stationery and pencil
ration card
identity card
birth certificate (if possible)
Bible or New Testament

BOYS

gas mask
1 overcoat and Mackintosh if possible
1 suit
1 pullover
1 hat or school cap
2 shirts (colored)
2 pairs stockings
2 under vests
2 pairs pants
2 pairs pajamas
1 pair boots or shoes
1 pair plimsolls
6 handkerchiefs
1 comb
1 toothbrush and paste
1 face flannel or sponge
1 towel
1 suitcase—about 26" x 18"
1 haversack
stationery and pencil
ration card
identity card
birth certificate (if possible)
Bible or New Testament

Finally, after what seemed an age but was, in fact, less than two weeks later, my mother sent us to bed early one night, telling us we would be going to Canada the next day. Overcome with excitement about the adventure ahead, we got about as much sleep as we did on Christmas Eve.

Chapter Two

*T*he soft noise of my sister closing the bedroom door made me rub my eyes sleepily, yawn, and stretch. Realization dawned! We're going today! I tumbled out of bed and rushed to the bathroom. Fully dressed, I ran downstairs to join my brother and sisters. As I started asking excited questions, Hazel put her fingers to her lips and pointed upstairs. Relishing the novelty of being up before my mother, I tiptoed out into the garden to play with the dog until breakfast time.

My mother made my favorite scrambled eggs on toast for breakfast, but I pushed it around on my plate, my stomach churning with suppressed excitement. Scolded, I made a face, and then managed to swallow it down with a big gulp of sweet tea after Margaret said that if I didn't, they would leave me behind. My father switched on the radio for the seven o'clock news. Our chatter stopped abruptly. Portsmouth had been bombed again, but fifteen German bombers had been shot down. It was going to be a fine day.

After breakfast, my mother and Hazel packed our sandwiches and the rest of us rushed upstairs, tripping over the steps in our haste to get ready to leave. When I came down again, my mother gave me a once-over. Freshly shampooed hair shining, light blue blouse tucked neatly into a dark blue skirt, white ankle socks, shining shoes—the picture of the demure, reserved child our escort would see. She helped me into my coat, straightened my badge, and then told me to pick up my gas mask and suitcase. The suitcases sat in an orderly row by the back door.

A bus was to take us to the nearest railway station to catch a train bound for Newport, the capital of the Island. There we would meet our escort and the other local children going to Canada.

I ran down the garden path to the front gate and peered anxiously up the road to see if the bus was coming. Eager to shout to the others to hurry up because they were late. I did not have the chance.

We waited in our coats with the big white CORB labels pinned on the front. We waited and waited. I hopped up and down, ran a little way up the road and stared. No one passed. Still the bus did not arrive. Finally, our parents realized we would miss the train. How would we get to Newport in time? With gas strictly rationed and most gas pumps removed from service stations, few people had cars. My father ran up the road to get the only taxi in service—a very ancient one. With all the able-bodied drivers in the forces, the taxi driver was even older than the car.

However, we all bundled into the old taxi with its cracked leather seats and its windows that didn't wind down and set off for Newport, a distance of twelve miles. Halfway there, it broke down. The poor driver, distraught, had no way of fixing it. Now what? We trudged to a bus stop and hoped a bus would come by in time. My aunt, who came along to give my mother moral support, muttered, "I think someone up there is trying to tell you something."

After forty very long minutes, a big green double-decker bus lumbered up, and we all climbed aboard. We had to sit downstairs because of our luggage. The other passengers—mostly middle-aged women clutching shopping bags—stared at the strange phenomenon of four young children, each carrying a suitcase and gas mask, and with a large white label on their coats. We missed the train at Newport, but the bus reached the pier at Ryde just a few minutes before our ferry was due to leave. We clambered on the little electric train that ran the length of the pier. The train was empty; everyone else had boarded the ferry.

The ferry, its two funnels belching smoke, stood at the end of the dock. A sailor with a large coil of rope prepared to cast off. The few other passengers hurried aboard, and a worried woman standing beside the gangplank with a clipboard in her hand, heaved a visible sigh of relief when we arrived. Ticking off our names on her clipboard, Miss Pinder, headmistress of the Gassiot Girls School in Ryde, told my parents she would look after us until we reached our port of embarkation. Our parents still had no idea where we were going to embark, or for that matter, on which ship we would sail, and they knew she could not tell them.

Turning to us, she said, "Hello, I'm Miss Pinder. Now, hurry up and say good-bye to your parents because the ferry is ready to leave."

We said a quick good-bye to our parents and then rushed up the gangplank to join the other CORB children waiting in a group by the rail. The gangplank was hauled up, the paddles started to churn, and we moved slowly away from the dock, waving good-bye to our parents. We looked at the rest of the group. Only eight other children from the Island. Miss Pinder told us we would be meeting other children on the mainland.

CORB, which organized our evacuation, forbade parents from traveling to the point of embarkation with their children. They reasoned farewells were traumatic enough for the parents at train stations. It could be overwhelming to see them sail away across an ocean for an uncertain number of years.

I beamed at my best friend and her brother and sister. I felt secure with family and friends along, but others were not so lucky. John Roberts, aged eight, was traveling alone. One of three boys, his younger brother was under five, and his older brother over fifteen, outside the acceptable age limits. His parents, however, had decided to send him to safety with an uncle in Canada.

Miss Pinder told us we could look around the ferry, but we must assemble at the head of the gangplank ten minutes before we arrived in Portsmouth. The old ferry with sidewinder paddles had wide decks on the main level, an observation deck on top, a saloon, a restaurant, and a smoking room. My brother explained to me, with the maddeningly knowledgeable air of a thirteen-year old, that it was an old ferry because all the modern motor-driven ones were now serving as minesweepers.

Hazel took my friend Jill Brown and me down to see the big steam-driven pistons. We pressed our noses against the protective partition, our breath fogging the glass, watching fascinated as the huge pistons slowly pounded away. Back on deck again, we leaned over the side, the wind whipping our hair back from our faces, to watch the seagulls diving into our creamy wake for scraps of bread being tossed overboard by a passenger.

As the ferry drew alongside the dock in Portsmouth, a major naval base, we stared in awe at a big aircraft carrier, gray and silent, slipping out to sea. Seamen, smart in their dress uniforms, lined the rail.

Ushered quickly from the ferry, we ran up the ramp to the station and slowed as we reached a platform packed with people. A cacophony of crashing boots, shouted farewells, barked orders, guards' whistles, escaping steam, banging doors, and shunting trains assaulted us. Hard on ears accustomed to a countryside only disturbed by the moan of the lighthouse's horn on foggy days.

Soldiers in khaki, with polished black boots, kitbags, and rifles on their shoulders, pushed their way to the trains. A few harassed civilians, an ashen-faced sailor with his arm in a sling, and another limping on crutches, tried to make their way through the throng.

A train pulled in with a screech of brakes. Compartment doors crashed against the side of the train as the people poured out. New naval recruits jumped off, kitbags on shoulder, and adjusted their hats to a jaunty angle. Wearing tight-fitting navy uniforms, bell-bottoms swinging, they pushed out their chests and swaggered off to join their ships.

On another platform, a guard blew a whistle, and with a hiss of steam and a jerk, a trainload of soldiers pulled away. Women waved handkerchiefs, and the men crowded their heads through the window to wave good-bye.

Our escort pushed her way through to platform number one, where we met another group of CORB children standing with their suitcases. The two escorts exchanged greetings and then bundled us into a carriage. The level of chatter rose as we excitedly introduced ourselves to our neighbors. People sat shoulder to shoulder in the packed carriages. The porter waved his flag, carriage doors slammed shut, his whistle shrilled, steam hissed and with a mighty jerk we pulled away from the platform. We were on our way to London.

As we slid and jerked along, more people climbed aboard the crowded train at each stop. At several stations, groups of three or four CORB children stood, clutching suitcases, with gas masks dangling from their shoulders. Some told us after they boarded that their parents gave them a last-minute chance to change their minds, but eager for the adventure ahead, they declined. Parents tried to smile bravely as they left. As the train pulled out, one hearty woman shouted, "Sing *Wish me luck as you wave me good-bye.*" The children who had just boarded, shy in front of their new companions, studied their shoes for a few minutes and then started asking the child next to them where he was from. The level of chatter, which had subsided at the station, rose again.

Not a single station had a sign showing its name. All station names, and indeed road signs, had been removed to make it more difficult for an invading army.

Our arrival at Waterloo Station in London and transfer by taxi to another station was a blur of packed bodies as we struggled down the platform and across the crowded concourse to a taxi stand in the wake of our stalwart escort. Outside the station, the traffic roared by, diesel fumes filled the air, and a long line of tired people waited for taxis. Reserved taxis quickly whisked us away. Jammed in the middle of the backseat, I could see very little through the windows. I caught glimpses of soldiers in khaki, nurses in dark blue uniforms, sandbags in front of big buildings, and people precariously riding bicycles amidst the traffic. We piled out of the taxi at Euston Station and struggled up the platform to a long green steam engine streaming smoke into the glassed-in station. We started a long, slow journey to an unknown destination somewhere north of London. Several times, the train jerked to a stop and shunted to a sideline to let troop trains rattle through. On a seat too high for my feet to reach the floor, I was nearly knocked to the floor by the shunting.

We arrived at a train terminal. A child shouted, "I know where we are—it's LIVERPOOL." Loud "shushes" came from all the escorts. The child looked around guiltily, probably expecting to see a spy with a black moustache and a slick of black hair on his forehead listening.

Buses took us to Holly Lodge, a private school set in twenty-five landscaped acres on the outskirts of Liverpool. We filed in through the big doors, our feet clattering on the stone floor, up a long staircase with a statue that caused gales of laughter to erupt from all the eleven- and twelve-year-olds. A nude statue, which displayed parts of the human anatomy not normally seen by children.

Reaching an assembly hall full of children, I stared. I'd never seen so many. On the stage, a teacher called for silence, and our incessant chatter stopped. The teacher then called out our names in alphabetic order, and we were told to greet our escorts. When my sisters' and my name were called, we stood beside another eleven girls in Miss Cumber's group. Everyone was divided into groups of fourteen or fifteen girls or boys—no mixed groups. Miss Cumber would be accompanying us to Canada. I assumed my brother was in a similar group of boys, but we lost sight of him.

The escorts, all volunteers, were men for the boys, women for the girls. Most wanted to serve their country, but others were looking for adventure too. Certainly not for the pay—escorts to Canada received $12 per trip, escorts to Australia, the princely sum of $24. Some Dominion High Commissioners in London approached nationals living in Britain and encouraged them to volunteer. For others, it provided a way of returning home if they had been stranded at the outbreak of war.

After a meal, we were shown to our bedroom, a classroom set up with a camp bed and a desk for each girl. Other girls and boys were not so fortunate. The girls slept in the gymnasium, and John Roberts, the eight-year-old traveling alone, recollected sitting on a camp bed in a huge hall with beds stretching as far as the eye could see. He sat there with his little suitcase " . . . feeling very fed up."

The next day, we received a green ribbon for our coats, a pink card with a group number on it, and an identity disc to wear around our necks. After a church service in the school hall, we spent the day in the grounds meeting new friends and playing games.

Isle of Wight girls in garden. Author front row center.

That night, the air raid siren wailed. I fell out of bed, very tired, and Hazel dragged me across the cold, damp grass to a shelter. Thumb in mouth, I looked up in wonder at the night sky. Searchlights swept the sky, picking out the ghostly shapes of barrage balloons floating above the city. Big gray shapes, legless elephants with inflated tails holding up cables that shielded the city from low-flying bombers. Every time the searchlight picked out the glint of metal on a bomber, the ack-ack (anti aircraft) guns opened up in fury. The sound was deafening. Whenever the guns stopped to reload, we could hear the distinctive throb of the German bombers' engines and the screech of fighters trying to drive them away from the docks.

We filed into the shelter behind other weary children and sat on the wooden benches that lined the walls. Once settled, an escort stood up, waved his arms, and shouted above the noise of the gunfire. "What shall we sing tonight? *Roll Out the Barrel?*" Everyone cheered, and we began to sing song after song at the top of our voices. The raid outside forgotten. The bare bulb hanging from the ceiling swung from the vibration of the bombs. We were just singing a rousing chorus of *Run, Hitler, Run, Hitler, Run, Run, Run* when the all clear siren wailed its long note and sighed away. The sky glowed orange from the flames of burning buildings, and the acrid smell of smoke filled the air as we made our way back across the grass to bed.

The next day, we were examined by an English doctor, and any child with an infection was rejected and sent home with his or her siblings. Our luggage was also inspected. The luggage inspection was probably for security, but it had a side benefit. Simon Marks of Marks & Spencer, a large department store, had donated $14,000 worth of children's clothes in case any child was not adequately outfitted. It was a kind gesture because some of the children came from the poorer parts of London, and others had been bombed the night before. All their belongings lost as the house collapsed and caught fire. Those bombed accepted gratefully, but even from the poorest homes, parents had managed to put together the required clothes.

A day later, a Canadian doctor examined us and again, some children were rejected. That night, we went to bed early as we were to embark the next day. The sirens sounded in the night, and we spent hours sitting in the cramped air raid shelter on wooden benches. However, next morning, we had breakfast at six and were taken to the docks by bus.

We filed into the docks past smart sentries in crisp uniforms, polished buttons and boots, and rifles at the ready. Once inside, we were given milk with a cake and a pep talk from Geoffrey Shakespeare, the Chairman of CORB. He looked tall and strange in his three-piece London suit, a bright, white handkerchief peeping out of the top pocket, and stiff striped shirt but he was a nice man who saw each CORB ship off and asked us to call him "Uncle Geoffrey." He gave encouraging words about our adventure and also told us to behave, as we were all ambassadors of our country. "And when things go wrong, remember you are British—grin and bear it."

Years later, he liked to tell the story of a seven-year-old who had just landed in Canada and was standing at Halifax station, crying her eyes out. An eleven-year-old came over to her and said, "Stop that sobbing. Remember, you're British." Amazed, she stopped.

We formed a crocodile and two by two walked to the ship. Smoke from the night's air raid hung over the damaged warehouses and workshops. Bone-weary firefighters with smoke-streaked faces walking off duty with heavy legs brightened when they saw us. So many bright young excited faces, ones who were sailing to safety, must have cheered them after another night of carnage.

The dock was a mass of humanity. Troops clattering along on the concrete, civilian passengers clutching suitcases, dock workers laden with tools hurrying to the ships. Steel clanged, drills whirred, welding arcs hissed, and staccato bursts of rivet guns filled the air as the round-the-clock repair of damaged ships took place. The salt-laden air was heavy with tar, rope, and diesel. A column of troops striding up the gangway of a large gray liner caught sight of us and gave us a thumbs-up.

Finally, we reached *SS Volendam.* Eight-year-old Alan Corbishley said, "Coo! It's big" as the side of the ship towered above us. A ripple of excitement ran through the crocodile. As we lined up at the gangplank, an escort gathered up our gas masks and ration books.

"You won't need these anymore." We all beamed. We hated the smelly gas masks.

Escorts rushed around, making sure we all kept moving. Young boys, fascinated by the dockside clamor, stopped to watch huge bales of cargo swinging out over our heads and down into the holds. Or engaged in furious arguments.

"I tell you that's a corvette not a destroyer."

"Don't be so stupid. That's not a German bomber over there, that's a Blenheim."

We smaller ones struggled up the gangplank, juggling teddy bears, suitcases, and cookies.

The *Volendam,* a luxury liner of 15,434 tons of the prestigious Holland America Line, was bound for New York via Halifax in convoy OB 205. The crew numbered 273. The 606 passengers included 320 CORB children, 2 doctors, 3 nurses, 26 escorts traveling with us, 15 children traveling alone or with their parents, and 271 adults. A total of 879. Rear Admiral G. H. Knowles, commodore of the convoy, boarded with his staff.

HOLLAND-AMERICA LINE.   ROTTERDAM - NEW YORK
VIA BOULOGNE-SUR-MER.

T.S.S. VOLENDAM. 15434 Tons Register- 25400 Tons Displacement.

SS Volendam

When Hitler invaded Holland, the *Volendam* was able to slip out
of Rotterdam before the city was taken. Operating under contract
to the British Ministry of Transport, their only stipulation had been
that the crew should remain Dutch. A fortuitous stipulation from
our point of view since they were a marvelous crew who treated us
well and were a model of efficiency.

Geoffrey Shakespeare, the Chairman of CORB, watched us
embark. In his memoirs, he said, "It was always a thrilling, if
mournful, experience to see hundreds of small children climbing the
gangway, clutching a bundle of luggage as big as themselves . . . We
were wise to make it a rule that parents should not accompany their

children to the port . . . It was heartrending enough for those who had never seen the children before." He felt it would have been unendurable for parents.

On one occasion, a member of the board, "a hard-headed businessman with little respect for politicians and less for civil servants" accompanied him. He continued, "We stood together to wave final farewells to a group of CORB children who lined the rails as the ship pulled away from the dock, singing *There'll Always Be An England.* I turned to pass a remark to him, and to my surprise, the tears were coursing down his cheeks . . ."

Many children had never even seen a luxury liner, let alone traveled on one. I was excited to be going on board one for the first time, but I had seen many large liners. Luxury liners passed by our bay on their way to the port of Southampton, so close that we could see the passengers on deck.

We were shown to a cabin, which I shared with my two sisters. Hazel looked around, checked, and nodding approvingly, said, "We've a nice bathroom." As soon as we had unpacked our suitcases, a stewardess came around and showed us how to put on our life jackets and then marched us up on deck for a lifeboat drill.

After the passengers boarded, the ship slipped away from the dock out into the Mersey estuary. Here, it anchored and waited for the rest of the convoy to form up. Ninety ships formed five columns with the *Volendam* positioned front and center of the middle column.

That night, we heard the wail of sirens, the throb of bombers, and the continual kerump, kerump of bombs as Liverpool suffered another air raid. The ship was in total darkness outside, but inside, lights blazed, and we ate luxurious meals. John Roberts said, "They've told us we can have ice cream every night if we want." Bliss.

At five in the morning on August 28, the convoy set off with a lone destroyer and two sloops to guard us. A sloop, a small, lightly armed vessel capable of only fifteen knots, was an efficient U-boat hunter. The escorts were far too few and too lightly armed to defend a convoy of this size. To defend a convoy effectively, seven escorts were needed for every twenty ships. However, in 1940, convoys of thirty ships had to sail with just one escort ship.

Destroyers could outrun and outmaneuver a U-boat, but the merchant vessels were generally too slow and too cumbersome to dodge torpedoes. After the fall of France in May 1940, the Germans were able to set up U-boat bases in Western France. A perfect launching spot for the U-boats, which now had the mid-Atlantic within range.

The navy had to guard the English Channel against the invasion forces and escort troops to the Mid East and Far East to defend colonies. Thus, we had to sail with what was available. With Britain in desperate need of food and oil, the merchant ships must sail. They would return with cargoes of wheat and packed with the Canadians who had flocked to enlist when Canada declared war on Germany just a few days after Britain. In fact, all the Dominions declared war within ten days.

When we set sail at the end of August 1940, the Atlantic battle was raging. In the four months of May, June, July, and August,

1,300,000 tons of British and neutral ships had been sunk. That is 351 ships. An average of almost three a day.

Totally oblivious to all the risks and looking forward to a new and exciting life, we set sail.

Chapter Three

"Come on, lazybones. Time for breakfast." Hazel's laughter-filled voice pulled me out of a dream. I sprang out of bed, narrowly missing cracking my head on the bunk above. As I rushed to the bathroom, the throb of engines tingled through my bare feet.

The dining room sparkled with crisp white linen, shining silverware, and bowls of fresh flowers. A waiter in a starched white jacket showed us to a table and gave each of us a gigantic menu. I scanned the bewildering number of choices and then took furtive looks at the other tables. Passengers tucked into plates filled with eggs and bacon. The strict rationing on shore allowed only one egg and two ounces of bacon per week; the passengers appeared to be eating more than their weekly ration at one sitting.

The waiter returned and set a pot of tea, a large rack of toast, and a dish containing enough butter to last our family an entire week in the center of the table. He turned to Hazel.

"What can I get you, madam?"

With a pleased blush, she ordered eggs and bacon. When it came to my turn, I sat up very straight and said in a clear voice, "Cornflakes and a boiled egg please." The waiter winked.

As we munched our way through the toast, a teacher stepped on to the platform at the end of the room and tapped the microphone. The chatter and clatter stopped.

"Good morning, children. After breakfast, it will be lifeboat drill. When the alarm bell rings, run to your cabins and put on your overcoats and life jackets. Wait in the gangway for your escort. He or she will take you to your assembly stations on the top deck."

When the bell shrilled a few minutes later, we ran to our cabin. I hurtled down the stairs and was there first. A stewardess waiting in our cabin checked our life jackets, and bustled us out into the gangway to wait for Miss Cumber. Within minutes, Miss Cumber arrived together with the rest of our group, and we hurried up to the lounge on the top deck. We found station number five, painted green, on the starboard side of the lounge. Around us, the other children assembled in untidy rows in front of their marked areas.

I hoped we would go to the lifeboats, but when a bossy, red-headed girl asked, Miss Cumber said in a loud, high-pitched voice, "We won't be going to the lifeboats today, but when we are dismissed, you can all go out on deck for the church service."

Once on deck, I craned my neck to look at the lifeboats strapped high above our heads. I was dying to explore them. With both ends the same shape, it was impossible to tell from below which was the bow or the stern.

A naval chaplain with a white dog collar led us in prayer, and of course, we sang *For Those In Peril On The Sea*, one of my favorite hymns. He gave a short sermon. Even that wasn't boring with the wind blowing in my hair, a fitful sun warming my cheeks, and gray ghost ships floating by. Afterwards, he told us to pray quietly for a few moments. Finally, he broke into a wide smile and said, "Now go and have fun on the decks." We remembered not to cheer since he was a chaplain.

Free to explore the ship, I hung over the rail and watched the sea change color as we moved away from land. The choppy blue-green water changed to the long, slow swells of the Atlantic and turned deep gray. Nothing but the throb of engines beneath my feet and long, gray lines of silent merchantmen all around. Gray sky, gray sea, and ghostly gray ships. Liners, long, low tankers with cabins and smoking funnels astern, unwieldy cargo ships wallowing in the long swells, and fussy little rust-streaked tankers bustling to keep up. The grayness was punctuated from time to time by winking lights as the merchantmen, under radio silence, communicated by signals. As the ships steered a zigzag course to lessen the target for submarines, they passed close enough to let me wave to passengers on other ships. From time to time, the escorting destroyer—blue ensign flying, big guns swiveling—steamed up and down the lines, causing a buzz of excitement.

On our ship, important looking officers in smart uniforms strode toward the towering bridge. Stewards patrolled the decks, tucking rugs around the legs of elderly passengers and bringing them steaming mugs of beef tea.

Below decks, it was easy to get lost in the long gangways running between cabins and the stairs leading to other decks. Negotiating our way from the cabin to the dining room would have been difficult enough under normal circumstances, but with all the watertight compartments in place, it was a maze. The compartments—massive steel structures with doors that had clanged into place once we left the safety of land—blocked off obvious routes, causing us to retrace our footsteps. However, with the help of stewards and escorts, we soon found our way around.

Children ran around the ship, exploring and meeting new friends, totally oblivious to danger. This disregard for danger presented a worry to our escorts and the ship's crew. Each escort, aided by guidelines drawn up by the Ministry of Shipping, set out some basic rules that we must follow:

Do not climb on the ship's rails.
Do not put your head out of the porthole.
Do not go on to the upper deck at night.

In order to keep us occupied and out of mischief, the escorts organized games. We played table tennis, deck games, and board games like ludo and snakes and ladders. We all loved the singsongs, belting out *Ten Green Bottles, Yes, We Have No Bananas,* and *There'll Always Be An England* at the top of our voices. With the wind carrying our voices away, we didn't have to worry about disturbing other passengers. Our favorite game was shuffleboard, a complete novelty and easy to learn. You simply pushed discs into marked areas and tried to push your opponent out. We played it with great vigor, the salt air whipping our cheeks to a rosy red and the acrid smell of coal-powered steam blowing over us.

Running round the wide decks was fun, but the best was peering through the rails on the stern of the ship, watching the huge waves, creamy with foam, fanning out in an ever-widening line behind us. On the first day out, seagulls followed, squawking and diving for jettisoned trash. But they disappeared when the gray green of inshore waters turned to the dark swells of the Atlantic.

After lifeboat drill next day, most of us went autograph hunting. Clutching our multicolored books in one hand and a stubby pencil in the other, we accosted everyone we saw. With children from Scotland, Wales, and other parts of England, and the crew with strange Dutch names, it was far more fun than at school.

We had to wear our life jackets wherever we went. At least, we no longer had to take our tiresome gas masks with us. We all hated them. Ugly black things with snouts like pigs, they smelled of rubber and felt claustrophobic. The government worried that Hitler might use gas warfare—the dreaded mustard gas had been lethal in WWI—issued gas masks and insisted that civilians carry them wherever they went. For children under five, some genius came up with a Mickey Mouse gas mask, but mature six- and seven-year-olds had to have a smaller version of the ugly adult one.

At dinner time, the wind rose, and the ship started to roll. Dishes slid around the table, and the stewards had to balance themselves on the sloping deck as they rushed between the galley and the tables. I began to feel queasy. A stewardess promptly took me to my cabin. She had blonde hair, swept back and clipped into a whirly thing at the back. At five six or five eight, she seemed a giant to me since my mother was five feet nothing. I was hauled along the gangways, my arm stretched to the maximum, while other stewards grinned at my escort, knowing they too would soon be doing the same. Once in my cabin, she tucked me into bed and brought me tea and toast.

That night, preparations were under way in the dining room for the next day's celebration. Stewards hung decorations, put balloons and flowers everywhere, and placed little Dutch flags on all the tables. It would be the birthday of Queen Wilhelmina of the Netherlands, and a cause for Dutch celebration.

All the young children were given presents. My friend Jill received a doll, and I was given a small toy panda. Pandas were a novelty in 1940, so it was a rare treat. My eldest sister, Hazel, brought mine to the cabin for me and told me about all the fun we would have the next day.

Meanwhile, as I learned later, two U-boats stalked the convoy. They had lain in wait just off the west coast of Éire, a neutral country, and picked up the convoy as it passed. They traveled silently, far enough back to escape the notice of the escorts. They were patient.

Chapter Four

Oberleutnant Adalbert Schnee checked with the hydrophone operators and gave the order to bring the U-boat up to periscope depth. Sitting on the periscope's folding seat and operating the hand and foot controls, he pressed into the cushioning around the eyepiece and watched the sea change from almost black to deep green, light green, and finally translucent drops that parted to reveal a clear night. Swinging the periscope around, he confirmed the information given to him by the hydrophone operators: no destroyer close by. The ships silhouetted against the night sky were lined up like ducks in a shooting gallery. He surveyed the columns of gray merchantmen and saw a large liner, with two smokestacks, dominating the centerline. Perfect.

A smile flickered across his face as he estimated the tonnage. It had to be over fourteen thousand tons. He already held two Iron Crosses, and the tonnage of the liner would push him towards the Knights Cross that he craved.

Fiercely ambitious, he already commanded a U-boat at the age of twenty-seven. Having joined the Kriegsmarine as a seekadett at twenty-one, he quickly ascertained that the fastest way to obtain a command was in the U-boat flotilla. In the stuffy traditional branches of the service, he would probably have to wait until he was in his late thirties or forties before he became a captain.

U-boat

Led by the inspirational and hardworking Grossadmiral Karl Doenitz, the U-boat flotilla was the most innovative branch of the German navy. Doenitz had, since WWI, been convinced that U-boats were the key to defeating the powerful British navy. His fervor attracted talented young men to the branch, and in the first stages of the war, it was obtaining the success he had predicted.

Successful U-boat commanders needed skill, daring, and a sportsman's eye. The U-boat's best weapon was surprise. U-boats could not approach a convoy on the surface, and even at periscope level, the telltale wake behind the mast could give away their position. Once sighted, they had no chance against destroyers that could outrun and outmaneuver them. Thus, the U-boat commander must surface, line up his victim, and strike quickly. Without the benefit of modern electronic devices, the ability of the commander to evaluate a situation quickly and take decisive action was key.

The whole crew depended on Schnee's decisions. No one else could see the enemy. Only he could decide when and how to attack. Launching torpedoes at a target in the ocean is far more difficult than firing a shell. The torpedoes sit in tubes that must be opened to the sea before launching. The sea swirling around them is far more unpredictable than air.

The British destroyers, equipped with ASDIC—an antisubmarine detection device—could detect U-boats under the surface but not at sea level. Like all skilled U-boat commanders, Schnee waited until nightfall, surfaced, and under the cover of darkness, mounted his attack.

Schnee estimated the distance between the submarine and *Volendam* and the speed at which they were both traveling. A ship's speed varies in accordance with its size and type, so Schnee estimated based on size, propeller speed supplied by the hydrophone operators, and course. He intended to surface and release his "eels" toward some point just ahead of the ship.

Schnee, with all the attributes required of ace submariners, had logged a series of successful strikes. U-boat commanders and crews were feted heroes on land, and Schnee, known as "the snowman" (Schnee is snow in German), was one of them. Something the good-looking young man used to great advantage with the ladies.

Schnee retracted the periscope as the U-boat neared the convoy. The periscope's telltale feather of water might be spotted by a lookout on one of the ships. He conferred with the chief engineer and decided that the only way to claim the largest prize, SS *Volendam,* was a frontal attack. With columns of ships flanking her on each side, the only way to get a clean shot was to surface, outrun the convoy, turn, and run straight at her, banking on the destroyer being too far away to prevent the attack.

Schnee took a bearing, calculated rapidly, and aimed at the soft underbelly of *Volendam.* The chief engineer gave a rapid string of commands, bringing the U-boat around in a complete arc. The well-trained crew, with complete faith in their young commander, set the depth and course bearings on the torpedoes.

Torpedoes are like miniature submarines with a fuel tank or batteries, propellers, a depth mechanism to maintain a set depth, and a gyrocompass linked to a rudder to maintain its course.

The hydrophone operators listened for the sound of the destroyer's propellers and gave the all clear.

"*Los . . . eins . . . zwei . . . drei . . . los!*" Two torpedoes released with a three-second interval sped toward the target. A simultaneous launch of two torpedoes would upset the trim of the U-boat, so Schnee turned this disadvantage to an advantage. He fired the first torpedo to create a large hole and the second one to go in through the hole. The second torpedo explosion would break the ship in two. *Volendam* would sink within minutes.

The submarine shuddered from the shockwave as a torpedo struck the liner. The crew let out a spontaneous, muted cheer.

Schnee watched fascinated as a huge pall of black smoke rose over *Volendam*, and flames began to lick her side. The hydrophone operators shouted a warning, "Destroyer approaching."

Bitterly disappointed at being deprived the satisfaction of watching his prize sink, Schnee swung around and saw the destroyer bearing down on them.

"Dive! Dive!"

Chapter Five

S S *Volendam* shuddered as the torpedo struck. Below decks, torn metal screamed, wood partitions shattered, and shrapnel flew in all directions. In our cabin, the lights failed, drawers flew open, hairbrushes and a traveling clock crashed to the floor. Our suitcases slid across the wooden floor as the ship listed to starboard. The abandon-ship bells sounded. I slept on.

Two days out to sea, two hundred miles from the nearest land, at 10.30 p.m., we had to abandon ship. Fortunately, my eldest sister, Hazel, heard the explosion and well aware of what this meant, got out of bed. In spite of the darkness, she was almost dressed by the time the alarm sounded and the lights came on again. Margaret, roused by the alarm, jumped out of the top bunk and dressed quickly. Hazel, fastening her life jacket, shook my shoulder and told me to get up. Rubbing my eyes and yawning, I climbed out of my bunk. "Off to the bathroom, and be quick. We have to hurry to the lifeboats."

By the time I had visited the bathroom, she had my clothes laid out for me and helped me clamber into them. Just as she was buttoning up my stays, a strange little warm undergarment, the stewardess came in. She looked approvingly at the other two wearing their overcoats and life jackets and said, "Just put on her overcoat and life jacket. She'll be fine. The other children are already waiting outside."

The stewardess tied up my life jacket and ushered me unceremoniously through the door. In the gangway, the rest of our group stood bundled up in overcoats and life jackets. Some of them were rubbing sleepy eyes, and all had tousled hair. I blinked as fumes stung my eyes. Miss Cumber smiled at us and then counted the group.

"Okay, children, we're all here. Let's go up to our assembly station."

She set off at a brisk pace and I found I was almost running to keep up. As I hurried along, I could feel the fumes at the back of my throat. We soon caught up with the group ahead. Together, we all began the climb to the upper deck, bumping along as our life belts touched the person in front of us.

The lounge was a sea of orange with children standing in neat rows behind their numbered, colored lifeboat stations. I stood fascinated by the scene as one by one, the groups filed out of the lounge. It was fairly quiet as most of the little chatterers watched sleepy-eyed. Miss Cumber counted us again, and then we waited patiently for our turn to go to the lifeboats. Fully awake by now and impatient for my turn, I watched each group in their bright orange life jackets follow a steward out to the deck.

Nobody was crying or frightened as we all knew exactly what to do. Lifeboat drill was part of our routine and not unlike going to the shelters at school. Eight-year-old Alan Corbishly said, "I thought it was only practice at first, but I didn't mind even when I knew we had been hit." We were all far too interested in what was going on to be frightened.

Below decks, stewards ran through the cabins, checking for children. All the children were in overcoats and life jackets and at their stations within three and a half minutes of the alarm sounding.

One seven-year-old, who did not wake up, said, "The cabin steward collected me in my pajamas, put on my overcoat, and wrapped a blanket round me. He carried me up to our lifeboat station."

Another girl awoke to find her two sisters had already left. She clambered into her clothes and rushed to the assembly point. "When I got there," she said, "I gave them a piece of my mind, I can tell you."

The Captain later wrote in his report, "As regards the conduct of the passengers and crew, everybody remained calm. There was no panic whatsoever. The children went to their assembly places in perfect order, and I must say their conduct was inspiring. I greatly admired the way they behaved."

"I saw British pluck at the age of five," said a twenty-year-old British seaman. "One would have thought that boys and girls, roused from their beds, rushed up on deck, and passed into lifeboats, would have been afraid. What did these kids do? They sang *Roll Out the Barrel* and kept on singing until they were safely on board rescue ships."

A woman on board another lifeboat remembered feeling scared until she heard children singing in one of the other boats. "The sound of cheerful voices coming from across the waves took all my fears away."

The lounge cleared quickly. When our turn came, the stewardess ushered us to the lifeboat as if she were simply loading an excursion bus. Outside, the wind howled, waves crashed against the side of the ship, and seamen's feet thudded as they ran to repair damage. The air was heavy with salt, mingled with smoke from the fires in the bow, and sporadic showers lashed our faces. I looked in amazement at the brilliantly lit decks and leaned into the wind as I followed the stewardess. Beyond the lights, the sea looked black. I watched a group of seamen struggle to manhandle a lifeboat from the port to the starboard side. The ship's list was so extreme, it was impossible to launch boats on the steep port side.

Two lifeboats were being lowered, and the children's singing competed with the sound of the wind and waves crashing against the side of the ship.

A steward, grinning reassuringly, picked me up and deposited me at the bottom of the boat along with the other younger members of the party. I could not see over the tall sides, but I looked around and found I knew quite a few of the other children. Four seamen clambered in after us, and the lifeboat swung out over the side of the ship. We moved slowly down the massive side, slick with water, past blacked-out portholes.

The lifeboat, thirty feet in length, open to the elements, and clinker-built (planks overlapping each other) had a point at each end, very much like a Boston whaler. Painted white, it was equipped with oars and a small sail. Two seamen manned the oars, one the tiller, and the other let out the ropes as we went down the side of the ship.

As we hit the water, a wave grabbed our boat and hurled it against the side of the ship. Waves pounded us against the side of the ship time and time again before the crew could release the lines. Finally, we pushed off into the path of a towering black wall of water. As an eight-year-old said so succinctly, "Coo! It's big."

The men on the oars dug into the sea as we pulled away from the ship. Their leg and arm muscles rippled as they fought to keep the bow into the oncoming waves and to get away from the sinking ship as fast as possible. They seemed to be pulling up the side of Everest. The waves, which appeared to be big swells from the deck, looked like black mountains from the lifeboat. I popped my head up to look over the side but ducked back quickly as freezing spray cut into my face.

The boat climbed up the side of a wave, through the white breaking crest whipped into fury by the rising gale, and then slewed down the other side. As we slid to the bottom of the trough, my stomach and that of every other passenger went with it. I started to feel very sick. The boy next to me threw up.

I learned later that all eighteen lifeboats were launched with speed and efficiency. None shipped any water, a remarkable feat, and only one casualty marred a perfect launch. The purser (the ship's administrative officer), fell between a lifeboat and the side of the ship as he climbed down a rope ladder to the boat. Before anyone could rescue him, he was washed away. Another crew member sustained a severe injury to his wrist during the launch of the lifeboats but insisted on rowing to a rescue ship and helping transfer the children aboard. When he reached the deck, he passed out from the pain in his wrist.

A child traveling to New Zealand on board the *RMS Rangitata* in the same convoy said, "I was woken to thumping noises and the sound of alarm bells. We put on our life belts and stumbled our way to the boat stations on the first-class deck, on the way sighting the *Volendam* brightly lit and apparently on fire falling astern of us. We were told the ship had been hit. There were children on board we had been playing with just a few days before. The convoy was ordered to scatter. We felt the engines below throb as the ship gathered speed. It was probably a terrifying experience for the older children and adults, but I found it exciting. We lay on the deck just outside the lounge, wrapped in blankets."

Three small merchant ships, *Bassett Hound, Valldemosa,* and a Norwegian ship, the *Olaf Fostenes,* broke convoy and stood by to pick us up. They waited a fair distance from *Volendam* to avoid the dangerous suction her sinking would create. A searchlight from an escort vessel swept across the sweat-streaked faces of the oarsmen as they struggled to get us to a rescue ship. Pulling with all their might, they brought us closer and closer to the rescue ship, but it took almost two hours.

Once away from the lights of the ship, the sea turned a deep, dark gray. The night sky was clear except for squally clouds, but I could see nothing other than sea and sky. Overcome by seasickness, nothing seemed to matter. I just wanted the horrible slewing motion to stop. Looking around, I could see everyone else except the crew felt the same. Later, children in other boats told the same story. Eight-year-old Alan Corbishly said, "I was seasick . . . Everybody in the boat was sick. We had a doctor in the boat, but he was sick too."

I tried fighting the nausea by thinking of other things. I watched the seamen's strained faces as they dug their oars into the waves and hauled away. Everywhere else I looked, children and escorts were green-tinged or throwing up. With my head spinning, I finally leaned back against the side of the boat, closed my eyes, and hoped we would reach a ship very soon.

The helmsman yelled in Dutch above the screaming wind, *"Pull, pull! That poor bastard on the tanker is a sitting duck while he waits for us. There's a U-boat prowling. Pull, pull!"*

The captain of the *Valldemosa*, a small tanker, heaved a sigh of relief as our lifeboat pulled to the side of the ship.

Valldemosa

Once secured, the perilous process of transferring us from the lifeboat to the bucking deck began. Some older children clambered up the netting, but smaller children, still wobbly-kneed from nausea, were unable to make it. So two members of *Valldemosa's* crew scrambled down and tied ropes around us.

A tall, broad-shouldered seaman with untidy curly hair put a rope around my waist and said, "Hang on to the rope, titch." Then yelled, "Next one for the Skylark," and the men above hauled away. I landed unceremoniously on the deck, and an escort tore the rope off me and threw it to a member of the crew.

Meanwhile, on the *Olaf Fostenes*, a Fyffes banana boat, the problem of the transfer was solved by swinging the children on board in banana baskets.

My six-year-old friend Jill was distraught when she dropped her teddy bear as she swung up the side of the ship. She recalls it being the most traumatic moment of the whole experience. Fortunately, she was bundled inside a cabin, so she missed the sight of the lifeboat being cut adrift and sunk by an escort ship to prevent it from being a shipping hazard.

Once on board, chilled from the wind and freezing spray, we were offered hot pea soup. However, even hot tea and cookies did not tempt me. I just wanted to lie down to escape the dizzying effects of seasickness. The empty tanker's roll in the huge swells was marginally better than the lifeboat, but a strong smell of diesel pervaded the ship. My stomach did not settle.

The captain gave up his cabin, a large room with a carpet, big bed, and a wash basin. Packed in like sardines, some children, including my sisters, slept on the bed, while the rest of us slept on the floor. I was comfortable with my life jacket as a pillow and a coat to keep me warm. Wedged between two other children, I didn't roll as the ship pitched. Lying down with my eyes closed, I felt better and fell asleep.

The small crew did everything they could for us. One even threw in candies, a rare treat in days of rationing. However, no way could I face a candy. I remember vividly lying on the floor for two days clutching a toffee wrapped in cellophane.

The *Valldemosa,* a ship with accommodation for twelve, took 250 survivors on board. Every bunk, cabin, companionway and lounge was cluttered with a mass of people. The extra weight caused the ship to settle so low in the water, amidships was permanently awash. No one complained. The ship's galley cheerfully ran a nonstop service of hot drinks and distributed chunks of bread, butter, and boiled eggs. The *Olaf Fostenes,* a freighter designed to carry fourteen persons, picked up another 250 passengers.

With the passengers safely away, the captain of *SS Volendam* set about saving the ship, and the destroyer pursued the U-boat.

Chapter Six

The destroyer's searchlight swept the water as Oberleutnant Schnee yelled "Dive" and hit the alarm button. Bells shrilled below. The two lookouts leapt through the hatch in the conning tower, slid down two ladders, and landed with a thud on the deck plates of the control room. The officer of the watch followed, and after him, Schnee lowered himself through the hatch, lifted the cover, and swung it shut above him. Stepping down a few rungs of the ladder, he spun the horizontal hand wheel to secure the hatch then slid at full speed down the rails to the control room.

The crew scrambled to their stations as the chief engineer prepared the submarine to dive. He closed the air induction and exhaust valves for the diesel engines that propelled the submarine on the surface and switched off the engines. The silent, battery-operated electric motors took over. All air vents were closed, and the vents to the ballast tanks opened to let the sea water in. The air, which gave the U-boat buoyancy, was expelled in a deafening roar. The submarine's nose dipped, and within half a minute, the conning tower had slipped beneath the surface.

The roar of escaping air ended to be replaced by a merciful silence broken only by the whirr of fans and the soft hum of the electric motors. The chief engineer took the submarine down to 130 meters and whispered instructions to the men controlling the hydroplanes to level the vessel. The submarine crept along silently at eight knots, her maximum speed beneath the surface.

With involuntary glances upward and a few silent prayers, officers and crew held their breath as depth charges thudded overhead. The U-boat shook with the vibration of the explosions but sustained no damage.

The U-boat remained submerged, and the crew waited. The air grew noxious. The crew perspired as the temperature rose, and shook their heads to dispel the dizziness and headaches that came as the oxygen in the hull slowly turned to carbon dioxide. Those not on watch lay on their bunks, trying to sleep to conserve oxygen. The only oxygen available was contained in the hull. Only returning to the surface could replenish it. Commands were whispered. The muscles of those operating the controls grew stiff as they used minimal movement. Explosions rocked the submarine from time to time, but these were farther away.

The minutes ticked by as condensation streamed down the walls and the air grew foul. External pressure in the deep prevented the one toilet aboard operating, and the noxious smell of urine in the buckets the crew had to use added to the odor of diesel oil, past cooking, unwashed bodies, chlorine, and stale bilges.

U-boats are weapons rather than vessels, and the crew had to fit themselves around the weaponry and stores. This meant cramped and uncomfortable accommodation. Submariners on different watches even shared bunks by crawling into a bunk their shipmate had just vacated. They could not bathe or take a shower and lived on a diet of reheated dried or canned food.

In spite of the well-known hardships, they had all volunteered for the U-boat service because a camaraderie, team spirit, and democracy not found in traditional branches of the navy existed. The terrible conditions, their vulnerability, and their shared responsibility engendered comradeship across ranks. This in turn ensured high morale. Each man was essential to the operation of the vessel, and one weak link could cause the death of the whole company. So whatever their role, they were respected. Men who were incompetent or not prepared to pull their weight were quickly weeded out of the service. Proud, happy crews put up with the appalling conditions for the hero status they enjoyed between missions.

U-boat hero Schnee, center

After three long, nerve-wracking hours, Schnee took the U-boat up to periscope depth. He swung himself on to the metal bicycle-type seat that straddled the periscope, leaned forward, pushed his forehead into the rubber cushioning around the eyepiece, and actuated the hoist motor. The motor hissed quietly, and he adjusted the focus. He stared out into the dark ocean, seeing nothing but black, but then the color slowly turned to dark green, then a soft yellow green, and suddenly he was looking out at the moonlit ocean. A wave washed over the periscope, leaving droplets of water that hampered his vision. He rotated the periscope 180 degrees. The sea was empty. The sloop and destroyer had given up the chase. Convoy and escorts had moved on.

With a sigh of satisfaction, he ordered the chief to surface and once there, the diesel engines were turned on, and lookouts clambered to their places. As wave after wave crashed across the hull, and the wind screamed around them, the lookouts on the narrow deck only a few feet above the sea, washed in the best of weather like a rock at half tide, hung on for dear life. The crew below gulped down huge breaths of fresh, clean air to expel the carbon dioxide from their system, and moved their cramped limbs.

Schnee looked at the rain squalls sweeping the deck and the mountainous seas powered by a force-eight gale and decided that pursuit of the convoy was impossible. He decided to look for easier prey.

Chapter Seven

*L*egs braced against the shock wave that rolled through the ship, vision obscured by the water cascading over the bridge, the Captain swung his binoculars around, and, as his vision cleared, saw a column of water crash onto the foredeck. Smoke and flames poured out of holes on both sides of the ship.

He rapped out orders. "Alert the convoy! U-boat attack. Assess damage."

At the siren's shrill, the convoy scattered. Engines throbbing, wakes churning, they powered away from *Volendam* to all points of the compass. Large ships, no longer constrained by convoy rules to the snail's pace of the little merchantmen, sped away, able to outrun any U-boat. The smaller ones, smoke stacks streaming, crammed on power until their plates shook.

The destroyer, *HMS Warwick*, rushed to *Volendam*'s aid. Her searchlights swept the sea, seeking the U-boat. Three small ships, *The Olaf Fostenes*, a smart banana boat, *the Valldemosa*, a rust-streaked tanker with a large rear funnel, and the *Bassethound*, a tiny tanker with its lower deck constantly disappearing under the swells, stood by, ready to rescue survivors. Messages blinked between the ships.

The *Volendam's* deck lights illuminated a hive of activity. Crews ran to ready the lifeboats. Seamen raced around, assessing damage. The Chief Engineer plunged down to the engine room.

The Captain listened as the reports from below rolled in:

"Hole fifty-four feet by thirty-two feet, sixty feet from the bow on the port side, sir. Over twenty smaller holes on starboard side."

"Ship afire on foredeck."

"Water pouring into holds one and two. Pumps started."

"Water flooding through ventilation system swamping C deck and crew's quarters."

Binoculars constantly sweeping the black sea, he paced up and down until a few minutes later more reports came through.

"Hatches battened down. Sluices and ejectors closed. Watertight compartments closed since port still holding, sir."

"Pumps in holds one and two not coping with water, sir. Water seeping into hold three."

"Bulkhead between two and three under pressure and in danger of collapsing. Pumps switched to keep hold three dry." The Captain cursed under his breath.

The First Officer standing at his side said quietly, "Water still pouring in. B deck flooded."

Jaw clenched, the captain looked at the rising sea—already at gale force six—and checked the falling barometer. He conferred with the Navigation Officer beside him. Worse weather was on the way.

Knowing the bulkhead between holds two and three could not withstand the sea pressure of a gale force eight, he shook his head. As hold three flooded, the ship would go down by the head, turn turtle, and sink. The First Officer turned to him and nodded. The Captain said, "Okay, sound the abandon ship. We need to get the passengers off."

A huge gust of wind and the Chief Engineer came in to join the Captain on the bridge. "Engines fine, sir. Auxiliary turbines turning. Two greasers below keeping an eye on them." The two men exchanged glances, both knowing the greasers had little chance of survival if the ship went down.

The Captain scanned the floodlit deck and saw orderly rows of children in their little orange life jackets marching quietly to the lifeboats. The Chief Engineer following his gaze said, "Christ, you'd think they were off to a school picnic." The Captain smiled for the first time since the explosion.

He watched the seamen lowering the lifeboats fight to keep them level alongside the swaying, tilting ship. First, the children, then the women, and finally, the men. The Deck Officer later told him with a grin that the ship's nurse refused to leave with the women, preferring to stay with her male patient.

The Captain noted with satisfaction *HMS Warwick* training her searchlights on the lifeboats that looked ridiculously small in the enormous Atlantic swells. Feeling the ship's list and lowering of the bow, he scanned the waves and decided he still had a chance of saving the ship. He called the First Officer, Chief Engineer, and Navigation Officer over.

"I think we can save her. She won't go down for a while, and the wind's rising, but shouldn't be too bad for an hour or two. What do you think?"

The First Officer walked over to the far side of the bridge and stared out at the sea.

"The engines can get us there. We've got them pounding away, and just as long as those pumps keep working, we can keep them above water." The Chief Engineer nodded. "Yes, let's go for it."

The Navigation Officer said dubiously, "The wind's working itself up to a force eight, but we do have a few hours to work with before it hits."

Returning to the group, the First Officer said, "We can regain the trim by pumping oil from the port to starboard side, but the real problem is going to be that bulkhead between holds two and three."

"Yes, the minute we start making way, the water pressure will crush that partition and hold three will flood . . ." The Captain stroked his jaw.

"And," added the Navigation Officer nonchalantly, "we'll go down by the head, plough into a wave, and not come out the other side."

"Okay, we'll pump the fresh water from the forepeak tanks overboard and move the rest of the fresh water and some ballast aft to bring the bow up so that damn great hole is mostly above the waterline." The First Officer looked pleased with himself.

"Yes, but don't forget that even if we can keep her afloat, she still has to sail two hundred miles to land."

The Chief Engineer interjected. "Those winds will whip the waves up, and there's no way the partition between holds two and three will withstand the pressure. Once that goes, three swamps, and we're on our way down."

"Not if we swing her around and go stern first. Do you think we can get some tugs to come this far out and give us a hand to bring her round?"

The Captain walked over to the communication tube. "Sparks, send off a message to the Clyde and ask for a couple of tugs."

The Chief Engineer raised an eyebrow. "I can't see tugs coming this far with a force eight brewing. They spend all their time puttering around in coastal waters. That's what they're built for."

"Yes, and your engines are built to go ahead for a few hundred miles. Not full astern. Reckon you can make it?"

The Chief Engineer shrugged. "Piece of cake."

"We'll see what Clyde has to say," the Captain said. "They're gutsy men those tug skippers. Can you imagine having to maneuver around ships our size without getting chopped in two?" He swung round to the First Officer. "Meanwhile, get all those holes shored up, and shift the ballast around. Tugs or no, we'll make it."

The seamen worked feverishly but found it impossible to shore up the huge hole near the port bow. However, many of the holes on the starboard side were only a few feet wide, and the crew hammered and welded until they were watertight. Damaged hatches were repaired and replaced, and firefighters succeeded in quelling the fires. The greasers in the engine room continued to joke and laugh as they sweated over their charges and kept the turbines turning.

The Captain relaxed as slowly the *Volendam* began to regain her trim and heaved a sigh of relief as the bow came up.

Two tugs set out from the Clyde through Atlantic swells whipped to a boiling fury by the gale. To add to their jeopardy, a stray U-boat might at any time surface and blast their undefended decks to smithereens.

The tugs pugnaciously punched their way through wave after wave, screws shuddering and decks awash. Finally, at dawn on August 31, they sighted the *Volendam*.

The liner towered above the tugs as the crew shot a light rope with a weighted end to the tugs. A routine operation in good weather, but with the tugs bucking and rolling in the heavy sea, and the wind hampering the line, it fell uselessly into the water. Time and time again, the line was shot, but each time, it missed its mark and fell into the waves. An impossible task. The crew on *Volendam* watched in dismay as one tug signaled good luck and turned back to port.

HM Tug Salvonia, with a naval crew on board, continued to stand by and when everything seemed lost, solved the problem. She came alongside the liner and a seaman with a line wrapped around him jumped across to a ladder on the ship's side. He clambered up the ladder, clinging on as waves clawed at him and the wind threatened to blow him into the sea. Exhausted, he made it to the deck only to be greeted by "a ruddy great officer with a gun pointing at me." The officer, unable to see the tiny tug below the ship, assumed he was part of a German U-boat boarding party.

With the light line secured, a heavy line was winched aboard the liner and tied at the stern. The *Salvonia,* assisted by *Volendam*'s engines going slow astern, proceeded to tow the liner, stern first, to Scotland against the fierce wind and raging sea. The situation remained critical all through the long day as the water continued to rise below decks and waves hampered their progress. However, in the evening, the wind began to drop, and the sea became calmer. The chances of reaching port increased.

On September 1, salvage vessels from the Clyde met *Volendam,* and their experts found she was drawing fifty-four feet forward and fourteen feet six inches aft. Her shattered hull, way down by the bow, continued to ship water. The foredeck was submerged, the dining saloon already under three feet of water, and the pantries swamped. Pumps transferred from the salvage ships to *Volendam* helped stem the flow, and on Monday, September 2 she arrived at the Firth of Clyde in Scotland. Tugs came to her aid and beached her stern first in the sheltered waters of Kames Bay on the Clyde.

Getorpedeerd met 170 kinderen aan boord .Volendam voor reparatie in het droogdok

Hole in Volendam's bow

On September 3, a diver went down to assess the damage. He climbed in through the massive hole, saw the remnants of the shattered torpedo, and then stopped short. He shot back to the surface to report. The incredulous officer shook his head and ordered another diver to go back down with him. The second diver suited up and went down. Running his hands along the casing, he confirmed what the first one had seen. In the hold, an unexploded torpedo lay inside the massive hole created by the first torpedo.

The second torpedo was not reported in the press; it was far too valuable a secret to pass to the Germans. The Admiralty removed the major prize and sent it to their experts for analysis where it provided invaluable information about the design and operation of the U-boat torpedoes.

The facts were not made public for decades, and I only learned about it relatively recently. It was incredible to discover I had been living a charmed life for over sixty years. Had the second torpedo detonated, the *Volendam* would have sunk within minutes.

Many stories exist regarding the second torpedo. The official Admiralty report states that it was released too soon after the first one, and the warhead was displaced by the explosion of the preceding torpedo.

Others believe it was a dud with a note inside. A happy thought that one—maybe some enforced laborer in Germany had found a way of fighting back.

Many more believe it was an act of providence. All agreed it was a blessing.

The British Admiralty expressed the greatest admiration regarding the behavior of the crew. "Their Lordships have noticed with satisfaction the high standard of preparedness and discipline which resulted in the successful transfer of some 600 passengers, including 335 children, to other vessels with the loss, and that by accident, of only one life. Captain Webster is further to be congratulated on his good seamanship in eventually beaching his ship in Kames Bay."

The British government honored Captain Webster, First Boatswain B.L.Ruygrok, and the First Engineer A van Son with the prestigious OBE (Officer of the Order of the British Empire). Six other members of the crew received the Merit Cross, a decoration bestowed by the Dutch government in exile in London.

*   *   *

The *Volendam* was finally moved to dry dock in the Clyde dockyards, and after a year of repairs, it was relaunched in July 1941 as a troop carrier. She carried one hundred thousand troops to and from battle zones without the loss of a single life. After the war, the ship returned to its home port of Rotterdam.

Captain Webster sadly did not survive the war. Traveling as a passenger on board another ship on his way to take over a command, he was lost when the ship was torpedoed.

*   *   *

An intriguing mystery remains. In the Captain's account of the torpedoing to the Admiralty, he states that the ship carried a cargo of 1,350 tons of wheat. I feel it would be understandable if it stated that the ship was going to pick up a cargo of wheat in Canada, but to suggest that it was taking wheat from Britain, which was critically short of food, is unbelievable.

In September 1940, a Polish ship left a British port carrying Jewish children being evacuated to Canada. It also carried art treasures from Poland's national art gallery and gold bullion from the Bank of England. It is, therefore, probable that the *Volendam* carried a similar cargo, but due to wartime information restrictions, these were not listed.

Chapter Eight

*T*he next day, aboard *Valldemosa*, they counted us—188 children. The other children had been rescued by the *Olaf Fostenes*.

Later in the day, the Dutch survivors, undeterred by the torpedoing, celebrated Queen Wilhelmina's birthday. The celebration consisted of canned peaches and cream, which they carried with them from the *Volendam*, and a singsong. A far cry from the major celebration that had been planned but good fun nevertheless. Or so they told me.

I felt too queasy to take part, and the mere thought of food made me feel worse. So I avoided the peaches and cream and spent the day out on deck in the fresh air. Since many of the other children felt the same way, I did not lack company.

My brother, Basil, fit as a fiddle, had a great time on board. Quartered in the Wireless Officer's cabin, he was soon being shown how everything operated. The crew, pleased by his avid interest, showed him over the ship. The Captain told him that he would make a fine sailor. Glowing under the praise, he left the ship determined to join the Merchant Navy.

Seven energetic children formed The Lookout Club and took turns watching for U-boats. They stood at the rail, scanning the sea in all directions for thirty minutes and then handed off to the next member of the watch. Told to go inside as night fell, they protested loudly. A steward from *Volendam* listening to their protests and feeling sorry for the flurried escort came to the rescue. He asked the children to explain the problem.

A serious girl in round wire glasses and a pigtail said, "We've kept watch all day because we know the captain and crew are busy, and we want to help. However," her voice rose in outrage, "now we are being told to go to sleep. It's at nighttime that the U-boats come. We must stay on watch."

The steward thought a moment. "I know what we can do. I'll get some other stewards to join me, and we'll form the night watch." He looked around sternly. "Just you be back to relieve us at seven o'clock tomorrow morning." He looked at her bare wrist. "What are you going to do for a watch?"

A red-headed boy stepped forward and wordlessly showed his watch. "Good. Okay, now off to bed with you. See you in the morning." With a grateful smile, the escort ushered her charges inside.

Two days later, the red-headed boy from the Lookout Club, wild with excitement, yelled, "Look, land!" Everyone cheered as the low hills of Scotland appeared on the horizon. An hour later, another boy standing near the bow raised his arm and pointed. "There's a Sunderland!"

I felt a big surge of excitement as the plane made a long, low circle overhead. Lights blinked on the plane, and the bridge returned the signal. A grinning member of the crew told us they were asking if we needed any assistance. "We don't, of course, we're nearly there."

As we neared land, the waters grew calmer, and squawking gulls greeted us. At the entrance to the Firth of Clyde, a stream of gray ships lined up to enter the busy shipping area. We had to wait our turn as all ships had to be guided through the anti-U-boat boom at the mouth of the harbor. The ships ahead of us were all merchantmen, mostly tankers, some with parts of their superstructure damaged, others with shell holes above the waterline. Overhead, fighters circled, and a destroyer steamed up and down the line. I watched the ships coming and going, and gradually, my stomach settled.

The next morning, we had a wash in a bucket out on the deck, the first for several days. It felt good to dash water over my face that felt sticky with encrusted salt spray and grimy from dirt on the floor where I slept. Water had been shut off in the captain's cabin wash basin. With 250 people on board a ship provisioned for twelve, water was scarce. A dark-haired girl with blue eyes and a cheeky grin splashed me. I splashed her back, and immediately, all the other young ones joined in. It was great fun until someone's bossy older sibling told us to stop wasting water.

The pilot guided *Valldemosa* past the boom, and we steamed up the Clyde toward the large docks. Naval vessels and merchantmen sat at anchor, awaiting repairs. Across the water, we could hear the clang of metal and the rattle of drills from the docks.

An hour later, we transferred to a smaller boat which took us to Gourock, a small town on the River Clyde about thirty miles from Glasgow. From time to time, our small boat rocked from the wash of a large naval vessel as it powered past, eager to get back into action.

Our boat bumped to a stop beside the quay's massive piles. Thin green seaweed clung to the piles, and the air was heavy with the smell of fish and tar. Ropes from the quay were hurled aboard, and seamen made them fast.

The wharf buzzed with activity as ships loaded and unloaded, and the rattle of drills repairing damage competed with the gulls and the shouted instructions. We made our way along the wharf, navigating our way through coils of rope and picking our way around boarded off holes. Workmen with rolled-up sleeves and faces reddened by the elements put down buckets of cement and stilled their pneumatic drills to watch us walk by. Our long line of children in bright orange life jackets must have been quite a spectacle.

The quay rocked beneath my feet as I took my first steps on land and I acquired a rolling gait. A tall white-haired lady in a WVS (Women's Voluntary Service) uniform waiting to greet us laughed, "Don't worry. You'll soon get your land legs back again. You were just on that rocky old boat too long." Smiling at us all, she added, "Come on. We'll soon have you in a nice warm room with lots of wee goodies to eat."

I boarded a bus and bumped my way along the narrow aisle in my unwieldy life jacket. Sinking into a comfy window seat, I looked out at the town with its gray stone houses and a big church with a crown steeple dominating the skyline. Behind it, the low hills of Scotland rolled away.

"Come on now. Up you get. Let's get inside the cinema. Lots of people want to say hello."

We jumped off the bus and walked to the cinema watched by a crowd of people. Old men in overcoats with the collars turned up. Women in long drab overcoats carrying bulging shopping bags and small children in pushchairs stared wide-eyed with curiosity.

An eye witness said, "To see them walking past in their little life jackets made you feel terribly sad—until you saw their faces. They were all as cheerful as crickets."

The lobby of the cinema was packed with children. The nice WVS lady led us to a table stacked with white plates, thick white mugs, and large platters of sandwiches. Beside the sandwiches stood a row of big brown teapots and a steaming tureen of porridge. A lady with silver hair, a beautiful fair complexion with a scattering of freckles underneath a dusting of powder, and an accent I had trouble in understanding pressed a bowl of porridge into my hands. The bowl felt good on my cold hands, and the porridge tasted delicious. The first thing I had eaten in two days, I could feel the warmth going down all the way to my toes. A few minutes later, a little square woman with a big, squishy bosom and a happy face said, "Here you are darlin', have a sandwich." The sandwich made of doorstep slices of homemade bread and full of crunchy cucumbers, lettuce, and sliced tomatoes disappeared in minutes. She gave me another one. However, as she offered me a third one, the first lady said, "That's enough the noo, or the bairn will pop." The woman smiled her assent and then pushed closer to me. I breathed in a wonderful smell of baked scones as she delved into her pinafore pocket and pressed a shortbread into my hand.

While we ate, five men in smart suits arrived and a man with silver hair, who looked like a retired colonel, finally allowed several men with cameras and notebooks to come in. I recognized one of the men in a suit as Geoffrey Shakespeare, the Chairman of CORB, who had talked to us in Liverpool. He wandered around and talked to lots of boys. Finally, in answer to the reporters who had been pestering him he said, "The escape of the children is an act of God. There was a very special guardian angel watching over them . . . but they are all in great spirits. They are marvelous . . . Most of the boys I spoke to want to go again."

As we munched contentedly and basked in the praise of the adults, preparations were underway to provide us beds for the night.

Later, a man who was then working as a fifteen-year-old bellhop at the Bayview Hotel recalled: "One night, the staff were told to get all the bedclothes, blankets, and pillows down to the big lounge and lay out all the bedclothes as there were lots of rescued children coming in off a ship that had been sunk. They arrived at the hotel with their label tags still pinned on them. My heart went out to them. I'll never forget it even though some of them were not very far from my age . . . I also had to take a lot of bedclothes to a big hall called the Pavilion for lots more children who arrived there . . ."

We had sailed under the supervision of C.H.Hindley, the headmaster of a school in Newcastle. On his arrival in Scotland, he said, "Never in my life have I felt so proud of British children as I did of those 321 boys and girls from all over England, Scotland, and Wales. There were town boys, country boys, rich boys, and poor boys in the party and also, of course, girls, and their cheerfulness and courage in the ordeal which they went through are beyond all praise."

A local Scottish newspaper reported: *"Children were greeted by Lord Provost Dollan, chairman of the Scottish CORB. He gave a few encouraging words to the children. He remarked on what had been done for them by the people of the town and called for three hearty cheers for all who had been assisting. This was responded to with great gusto."*

Being the last group to arrive, we went from the cinema to the station where a train took us to a school in Glasgow. We arrived in a strange assortment of clothes, pajamas, underwear or fully clothed. Many of us without shoes, and no one with a hat. But we all still had our labels pinned on.

A newspaper article dramatized the situation: *"The U-boat did its fell work at night while the kiddies were asleep, so most of them were clad only in night attire and blankets when rescued . . .*

We were soon supplied with clothes donated by local voluntary organizations. I was given a blouse and skirt and long black woolen stockings that itched all the way home. My friend and I agreed that they were very kind people, but she was given "the ugliest dress I have ever seen." As some of the last survivors to land, the clothes selection had dwindled. However, it was marvelous to be able to take off our overcoats at last.

After sleeping on cots in a school gymnasium, we were taken out to play in a park in the morning. It felt good to be running around in the open on a surface that stayed still. In the afternoon, we played hockey in a field close to the school, and later, a BBC van arrived with reporters who produced a microphone and asked children to speak to their parents. My friend's sister, Jaqui, was the first to volunteer.

"Hello, Mummy. I hope you are listening. We are all safe and well. Expect to be seeing you again soon."

Next morning, Geoffrey Shakespeare congratulated us on our bravery and gave us labels with sprigs of white heather tied with tartan ribbon. The label read: "Warmest congratulations! We are all proud of your bravery. Good luck!"

A huge panic ensued when it was discovered that one little boy was missing. He had not been seen since we left the *Volendam.* Escorts were running to and fro checking lists, and the local authorities were horrified. Geoffrey Shakespeare, who was on his way back to London, turned around and returned to Glasgow. Everyone breathed a huge sigh of relief when a naval vessel radioed to say that the boy had been found and was on his way to port.

He had slept through the explosion and alarm bell, and woke up to find his cabin empty. He went out to the gangway, looked around the lounge and the deserted deck, and could find no one. He returned to his cabin and went to bed. In the morning, a crew member found him wandering around below decks, collecting pieces of torpedo as souvenirs!

We stayed at the school for a few days and enjoyed playing with our friends while transport was arranged. Rumors swirled. We all wanted to go to Canada again, and someone said we would be going to Liverpool to embark on the next liner. Others said we were going straight home first. I didn't much care either way. I was having a great time.

Chapter Nine

S everal days after we arrived in Scotland, the Purser's body washed up on one of Scotland's outer Argyll isles.

With every incoming tide, evidence of the Battle of the Atlantic strewed the western beaches of the British Isles. Flotsam such as a shoe, a sailor's hat, a bottle, a lifebelt, an oar, a toothbrush, a tinfoil packet of Nescafé instant coffee, part of a lifeboat, a teddy bear, a packet of Players cigarettes, and always a slick of oil. Among them on a Scottish island, the sole casualty from the *Volendam*, the Purser.

Tiree, only seven miles long and three miles wide, is a beautiful windswept island of wide, sandy beaches, craggy rocks, flower-strewn moors, one-story crofter cottages, and Iron Age relics. Very flat and low, it has been described as "the island beneath the waves." A place where, standing on the shore and looking out over the ever-changing sea and sky of the Atlantic, you are at one with the ocean.

The body was carried inland and identified as a Dutch sailor, Rijk Baron from Harlingen in Holland. A married man of fifty-one with two children. His body was treated with respect and, after a burial service attended by the residents of Tiree, was interred in a local churchyard.

After the war ended, the Purser's relatives in Holland were contacted, and they exhumed his body and took him home. On Tiree, to this day, his gravestone still stands, slightly askew, facing out to sea. Its inscription in Dutch, translated, reads:

Fallen

In the Service

Of His fatherland

Purser Rijk Baron

SS Volendam

Born in Harlingen

6 January 1889

Died at Sea

30 August 1940

A fitting monument to a brave man and to the kind souls who looked after him.

Chapter Ten

The next day, we set off on the long journey from Glasgow to London. Uncomplaining civilians sat on the overfilled train, squashed between soldiers clutching kitbags. Tired sailors put their heads back and seemed ready to fall asleep while pink-faced nurses in crisp uniforms sat bolt upright. Self-conscious young airmen, exposing white necks below their newly cropped hair, lined the corridor.

We climbed into a reserved carriage, and the escorts opened up the windows to cool the stuffy train. A warm wind, accompanied by black soot, filled the carriage as we pulled away from the platform. The train swept past a group of women standing at the end of the platform, waving handkerchiefs, and we were on our way.

In the countryside, Land Army girls picking up potatoes in an enormous field waved to the train, and we all waved back energetically. At small stations, passengers waiting for local trains stepped back as our express whooshed through. In an unidentified city, a siren wailed, and our escort rushed over to close the windows and pull down the blinds. We heard doors bang, army boots clatter, shouts, and a whistle. Steam hissed from the train as it clattered over the junction points, picking up speed immediately. It grew hot and stuffy, but sticky and uncomfortable, my woolen stockings itching like crazy, I still kept chattering and playing games.

After what seemed like hours and hours, we pulled into a London station. I climbed out of the carriage onto the crowded platform, where I could see very little except legs. The round dome of the station roof echoed with the noise of shunting engines, escaping steam, whistles blowing, shouted orders, and unintelligible loudspeaker announcements. Red-faced ladies, standing beside a huge urn, handed thick white mugs of tea to passing soldiers and sailors. As we reached the exit, a group of men with cameras and notebooks rushed over. They snapped lots of pictures, asked us questions, and interviewed two of the escorts. Hazel said we were sure to be in the newspaper the next day.

Outside the station, away from the smell of coal-fired steam, the air felt balmy and soft after the brisk Scottish weather. The escort hurried us aboard a waiting bus bound for a college on the other side of London.

From my window seat, I saw sandbags piled in front of buildings and a large green park where couples strolled hand in hand. People thronged the streets in the shopping area—smartly dressed businessmen and businesswomen, soldiers in khaki, newspaper boys on the corners, and nurses hurrying along in their dark blue uniforms and swirling red-lined capes. Barrow boys selling black-market goods disappeared down side streets when bobbies in tall helmets approached.

I peered out of the window, hoping to catch a glimpse of the horse guards as we passed Buckingham Palace. I loved the guards with their red uniforms, shining breastplates, and plumed hats. However, the palace with sandbags piled in front and soldiers in khaki at the gates looked strange. I whispered to Hazel, "Where are the horse guards?"

"They went to fight in Europe, and now they are defending the South Coast. But they wear khaki when they're fighting, not those fancy clothes."

The escort pointed to the flag flying over the palace. "The King and Queen are staying in London in Buckingham Palace. They refused to go to Sandringham or Balmoral where it would be far safer. Princess Elizabeth and Princess Margaret are staying there too."

I was puzzled by this and asked my sister why the King's children weren't being evacuated like us. "The King told us in his speech that if the people had to stay and fight, so would they. The princesses are setting an example."

I felt sorry for the poor princesses having to set an example.

We soon arrived at a college where we were served a very welcome hot meal and given a bath. It felt good to shed my clothes and step into the warm water. Only five inches of water in the bath tub though—that was the patriotic thing to do. It saved power. Even the King had only five inches of water in his tub! I giggled to think of the royal bottom in a little tub of water.

John Roberts, who had been feeling ill on the train, remembers the bliss of being put in a bed with crisp white sheets in the sanitarium and being looked after by a large-bosomed matron in a starched uniform.

When they counted us at bedtime, a child was missing. However, she was already on her way to London. The six-year-old from Basingstoke in the south of England had become separated from her seven-year-old brother on the platform in Glasgow, and missed the train. An escort spotted her looking lost, scooped her up, and brought her to London by the next train. The escort said, "She was a perfect brick. Not a bit upset at being separated from her friends, but she was very glad to see her brother again."

The next morning, it was another train ride to Portsmouth, on to the ferry, and the final train ride to Newport. Parents with edgy, anxious faces lined the station as our train pulled in. Children crammed their heads through the windows, waving and yelling "Hello, mummy!"

Catching sight of them, the parents' faces broke into broad smiles, and they surged forward. One lady dressed in a smart tweed suit and silk blouse patted her hair self-consciously, one eye on the newspaper reporters' cameras, as she stepped briskly across to scoop up her son. My mother stood stock-still, rigidly straight, until I ran up to her. She gave me a beaming smile, and her whole body seemed to relax.

Several years later, my father explained. When my mother was told the *Volendam* had been torpedoed, she passed out. Four children lost in one fell blow. My father had a terrible time trying to bring her round and convince her we were all safe. The statement had been: "The *Volendam* has been torpedoed, but all the children are safe." She passed out before the "but." I don't think that until that moment on the station, she truly believed we were safe.

She gave me a heartfelt hug, and then turned to my brother who was hot on my heels. Parents, children, and newspaper reporters surged around us.

We must have presented a ridiculous sight as we tumbled out of the train still wearing our overcoats on a warm September afternoon. Once these were shed, parents looked amazed at our odd assortment of clothes.

"What are you doing in woolen stockings?" This from my mother who was used to seeing me in nothing but short cotton ankle socks even in the winter. Listening to my explanation and question, she added, "No, you cannot take them off until we get home."

John Roberts's frantic parents caused a stir when they could not find him. Calm was restored when the boy who had sat next to him on the train said, "Oh, he got off at Wootten." John had simply alighted at his stop which precedes Newport and gone home. After all, he was now a seasoned traveler.

Reporters from the local paper crowded around us on the platform and interviewed children and parents. Articles such as the following appeared:

ISLAND EVACUEE CHILDREN SAFE

Thrilling Experience

"The children arrived at Newport Station at three o'clock on Thursday afternoon. Some of their parents awaited them at the Newport Railway Station, and as the train came in, the little

ones looked anything but shipwrecked passengers. They were smiling happily and lustily calling out "Hello, Mummy." A representative of "The County Press" chatted with the children, but his questions were several times interrupted by the appeals of the children to their parents to promise to allow them to go again when a ship was available . . . Some of the parents promised there and then that they should go if they wished it after thinking it over for a few days . . . Basil Cole, a sturdy lad of twelve, was very definite that he was going again and said he hoped they would be able to go on the same ship because the crew were "jolly good sorts," and the skipper had told him he would make a good sailor . . . Little Wendy Brown, aged six and the baby of the party, was still a little disconsolate at the loss of her favorite teddy bear."

The headmistress, Miss Pinder, who escorted the children to Liverpool, said, *"If you had searched the Island, you couldn't have found a nicer party. I only hope that this doesn't stop parents from sending their children. It is the first time that it has happened, and the navy will see to it that it doesn't occur again."*

John Roberts and his mother were interviewed at their home later in the day, and this resulted in the following article:

BACK FROM ATLANTIC RESCUE
Young Evacuees Want to Go Again

Back from the biggest adventure of his life—the torpedoing of the evacuee ship to Canada—quiet-voiced John Roberts, aged 8, is quite sure he wants to go again.

He got back home on Thursday with the other Island kiddies and told an "Isle of Wight Times Reporter" just what had happened this week.

"We were all in bed," he said. "It was eleven o'clock at night when the ship was torpedoed. We all had to go up on deck and put our life belts on. They had shown us what to do."

The children were put into lifeboats and picked up by an oil tanker . . . They were three days out of port and were immediately brought home.

It was the first time that John had been on a big ship, and he liked it, though he admitted feeling sick in the lifeboat.

And asked if he felt afraid, he replied, "Oh, no."

One of his most pleasant memories of the voyage was of ice cream. He was given it, he said, after nearly every meal. Now he is anxious to start again. His parents also want him to have another chance and have sent in an application.

His mother was also interviewed:

"I have been notified every two days. I knew that he was well cared for and he was thoroughly enjoying himself. I'm terribly grateful for all they have done; I have great faith in the local organizers, in the people in London, and, of course, in our navy.

I want him to go again as soon as possible, and I hope it doesn't put other people off sending their children. "

After the interviews were over, we boarded a bus bound for home. On the way home, we regaled my parents with stories of our adventure, but mostly, we wanted to know what was for dinner.

Chapter Eleven

*T*ucking into my second helping of apple pie and custard, it felt good to be home again. I had worked up a healthy appetite in the garden where, like all good citizens, we had been busy "Digging for Victory."

After the success of German submarines in WWI, Karl Doenitz, who was to become Supreme Commander of the German Navy, believed submarines were the way to defeat a nation with superior naval power. Britain, a manufacturing country which imported seventy-five percent of its food, could be starved into submission by an all-out offensive on its supply lines. As Germany expanded its army, air force, and navy in preparation for WWII, Doenitz requested two thousand submarines. Fortunately, his request was vetoed by Hitler, but with the several hundred already under his command, he unleashed an all-out U-boat attack.

To compensate for the lack of imported food, the Dig for Victory campaign began. British citizens, encouraged to grow their own food, converted lawns and flower beds to vegetable gardens. For those with no gardens, stretches of land in public parks were allocated to anyone who applied. Allotments became a common sight all over the country. Side by side, people cultivated their plots, digging, weeding, and leaning on their spades gossiping with their neighbor. London's famous parks sprouted vegetable gardens, and even the moat around the Tower of London became a vegetable patch. As some irreverent wit on seeing peas growing around the Albert Memorial, said, "What finer scarecrow could you have?"

My mother had completed the conversion of our lawns and flower beds during our absence. No longer kept busy cooking, washing and ironing for four children, she channeled her energy into the garden. Working outside was her way of avoiding the empty house and worrying about her four small mariners.

The lawn and flower beds had been replaced by long rows of potatoes, onions, beetroot, carrots, and peas. At the end of the garden, rhubarb grew happily protected by old upturned buckets with the bottom knocked out. The day after we returned home, helping my mother weed two long rows of carrots, I looked with dismay at the disheartening sight of weeds invading the peas. My mother grinned, ruffled my hair, and said, "Why don't you go and help your sisters pick the apples? They can probably use a young monkey like you."

I dashed to the apple orchard and climbed the trees, tossing apples down to my sisters who picked the lower branches and filled a large wicker basket with crisp new Bramleys and Pippins. Next, we carried the basket up two flights of stairs to the attic, where we laid the apples out evenly spaced on the wooden floor. In the cool of the attic, they would keep all winter. For the next few months, dessert would be baked apples, stewed apples and custard, apple crumble, apple pie, and apple fritters.

My parents had fortuitously planted plenty of apple, pear, and plum trees when they first moved into the house, and in 1939, they had added gooseberry, black and red currant bushes.

Food was strictly rationed. Initially rationed to prevent stockpiling and panic if the shops had empty shelves, it became a stark necessity as U-boats and the Luftwaffe devastated merchant shipping. All food was rationed, and portions were low. For example, for each person, the weekly allowance was:

> Sugar—8 oz
>
> Cheese—1 oz
>
> Butter—2 oz
>
> Margarine—4 oz
>
> Bacon and ham—4 oz
>
> Preserves—2 oz
>
> Candy—2 oz
>
> Eggs (as available)—1 egg per week or 1 packet (makes 12 eggs) of dried egg powder per month

Luxury items like bananas, oranges, and pineapples disappeared completely not to be seen again until after the war ended.

To compensate for the lack of oranges, nutritionists developed rose hip syrup to provide the Vitamin C essential for babies and nursing mothers. After one year of rationing, an analysis determined pregnant women and young children were not getting enough nutrition. So specially colored ration books, entitling the bearer to extra rations, were issued to pregnant women. The standard ration books for adults and school-age children were buff colored, the ones for pregnant women were green. In an era when being pregnant was kept extremely private and in the case of an unmarried woman, a cause for deep shame, the green ration books could be an embarrassment.

Large dogs were a casualty of rationing; few could provide them with enough food. Small breeds became popular, and many large breeds would have died out completely if the U.S. had not continued to breed them. I found out, long after the event, that the *Volendam* was carrying several breeds being shipped from top British breeders to their counterparts in the States. The dogs survived and returned home safely—not in the lifeboats but on board with the Captain and skeleton crew. It was fortunate they kept the dogs secret from the children, or we would have besieged them on board and probably have thrown our escorts overboard to make room for them in the lifeboats.

We were not to spend too many days playing at home. On the Monday after our arrival, my father received the following letter from the headmaster of the high school that my brother and middle sister attended:

Dear Mr. Cole,

The whole staff here were very happy and relieved to hear that your children had returned safely from their

attempt to journey to the Dominions, and hope that they have not suffered in any way from their experience.

Meanwhile, I am informed by the Education Office that they should return to school pending any further plans to evacuate them, and I am therefore writing to ask if both Basil and Margaret will be coming to us next week.

If I do not hear from you by return, I shall expect them on Monday next, and assure them of a very warm welcome.

I am,

Yours truly,

(signed) D.H.Greatwood

There was to be no malingering or pampering. Back to school and no nonsense! If it happened today, counselors would have been rushing around to check on us and arrange therapy.

* * *

Back at school, after interest in my adventure had waned, my friends broke into excited chatter about the things I had missed in the Battle of Britain. Mr. Churchill told us in June that the battle on the continent was over and the Battle of Britain had begun.

The German army, massed on the North Coast of France, waited to launch "Operation Sea Lion," the invasion of Britain. However, with the Royal Navy lining the south and east coasts of England, the

Kriegsmarine, crippled by the Norwegian campaign, lacked the fire power to support the invasion.

Hitler turned to Goering, whose invincible Luftwaffe had spearheaded the incredibly successful Blitzkrieg, and ordered an all-out air attack on Britain. He reasoned that with docks decimated, cities on the South Coast flattened, and a massive army ready to invade, Britain would realize the hopelessness of their situation and surrender.

Goering felt confident that with the Luftwaffe outnumbering the Royal Air Force by three to one—640 fighters faced 2,600 Luftwaffe bombers and fighters—he could defeat the RAF in four days. The Luftwaffe would then be free to decimate British naval bases and supply lines. Operation Sea Lion could proceed.

The highly accurate and effective Junkers Stuka dive bombers, which had wreaked havoc in Europe, began the attack. Channel ports and convoys were attacked to lure fighters out over the sea where they would be easy prey for the Messerschmitts.

However, RAF pilots in Hurricanes and Spitfires mounted a spirited defense, and the pilots in the sophisticated Messerschmitts were surprised by the superior maneuverability of the Spitfire.

Dogfights between RAF fighters and Messerschmitts occurred daily, and we had a front row seat. The Isle of Wight lay below the flight path of the Luftwaffe on their way to attack ports. The RAF fighters, intent on breaking up the waves of bombers before they struck the cities, attacked them over our heads. We watched entranced as RAF fighters screamed down out of the sky with guns blazing to attack the bombers, and the Messerschmitt fighters swooped down on the RAF. The sky filled with vapor trails, puffs of ack-ack smoke and weaving, diving planes.

After the raids, spent bullet casings littered the downs, and I would run out with my friends to collect them for souvenirs. Occasionally, we found live ones. These we took home and placed in a vice in my father's boat shed. The bullet head, extracted with pliers, was discarded, but the thin strips of cordite inside made fascinating patterns when laid out on a piece of wood and ignited. One of the boys hit the detonator cap using a nail and hammer, but we discouraged him hitting it again. The satisfying bang was liable to bring outraged parents running.

On taking office, Churchill gave his inspiring speech: " . . . All I have to offer is blood, sweat, toil, and tears . . . Let us, therefore, brace ourselves to our duties and so bear ourselves that, if the British Empire and its Commonwealth last for a thousand years, men will say, 'This was their finest hour.'"

The popular joke in response to this call to action was, "Okay, we're in the final now, and it's on our home ground!"

People responded with unprecedented fervor. Not just the RAF, whose defense of Britain is the story of legends, but everyone. We were all in this together, and we intended to win.

Volunteers flocked to organizations such as the Red Cross, fire service, Women's Voluntary Service, and Air Raid Precautions service. Women went to work in factories, on the land, and joined the WAAF, WRNS, and ATS. The Home Guard, always the butt of jokes, supplemented the army by building defenses and standing guard duty. Unbeknownst to the general public, within the Home Guard, special units of ten men very familiar with the local terrain were trained to operate behind enemy lines if the invasion happened. When first formed, the Home Guard was called the Local Service Volunteers, or LSV, affectionately known as the "Look, Duck, and Vanish Brigade."

Output of factories producing planes jumped phenomenally as factories began operating around the clock, seven days a week, and workers put in long overtime hours. The average monthly fighter production stood at 156 in 1940. This jumped to 340, 563, and 420 in succeeding months

A lifeboatman in a town on the South Coast saw a merchant ship on fire in the channel after a German attack. The voluntary lifeboat crew dashed out to the rescue and, as the local fire service fought the flames, saved the men on board.

Pilots and ground crews worked nonstop to beat back the bombers. Pilots flew as many as four sorties a day. When they ran out of fuel and ammunition, they flew back to base, and were back in the air within thirty five minutes. During that time, the ground crew inspected for damage, refueled, re-armed, gave a final inspection, clean, and helped the pilot back on board. Meanwhile, the pilot was debriefed and sometimes grabbed a mug of tea and a bully beef sandwich before taking off to meet another wave of incoming bombers.

A pilot remembered on a typical day being tapped on the shoulder by an orderly, "Come along, sir, come along. 4.30." Waking slowly in the pitch dark and cold hut, I put on my flying kit over my pajamas and went out to my plane. A fitter jumped out as I climbed into the cockpit. "Morning, Jones, morning, Dexter. Put my chute on the tail please." I checked all the instruments. Everything in perfect order. Helmet already connected. Everything ready for a quick getaway.

Returning to the hut, I saw another pilot fast asleep in a deck chair. I lay down and zonked out immediately . . . What seemed the next moment I woke with a start to see everyone pouring out of the hut . . . I could hear the orderly repeating. "Fifty plus bandits approaching from South East."

Bob shouted, "Scramble, Graham, you lazy bastard." I ran out to my plane, struggled into my parachute, and was pulled into the cockpit by the ground crew who already had the engine running. Helmet, straps, and gloves on, last-minute check, and then I taxied out to take off. It wasn't until I was in the air that I was fully awake.

On other days, between raids, pilots—some as young as eighteen—sat around on airfields playing cards or board games or lounging, all kitted up in their flying jackets ready to scramble. At the word, they raced to their planes, bumped down the airfield, and rushed to attack the waves of bombers.

On August 30, Goering, infuriated by an enemy that refused to lie down, stepped up the attack. From 1 p.m. onwards, successive waves of bombers crossed the coast at twenty-minute intervals. To break up the attacks, Fighter Command flew an unprecedented 1,054 sorties. Some squadrons flew four times and almost all at least twice.

The Luftwaffe launched simultaneous high and low level attacks on different targets to scatter the RAF. But the RAF had a sophisticated early warning system in place. German commands were frequently intercepted by Intelligence at Bletchley Park who had broken their code. Radar stations along the South Coast picked up the oncoming bombers and relayed information back to a highly coordinated central Fighter Command which plotted the battles and scrambled fighters from different airfields.

This efficiency, and the superior maneuverability of the Spitfire, dashed Goering's hope of a swift victory. In July and August, 248 German planes were shot down with the loss of only 148 RAF fighters. The efficiency still had some gloriously British touches. A WAAF operator in a South Coast radar station reported bombers approaching from France and then hunkered down in her underground bunker to wait out the raid. The phone rang.

A laconic officer at Fighter Command said, "Pop up to the top, will you, dear, and let us know what type of bombers they are."

Holding her tin hat on with one hand, she popped up like a mole and reported the awesome array of bombers going overhead.

At recess one day in the playground, an excited boy with flaming red hair and big ears told me about the attack on the radar station at Ventnor. As he spoke, waving his freckled hands around to illustrate each point, a group of children gathered. On August 12, the Ventnor radar station—the forward most station of England's early warning system, located high on the Isle of Wight's St. Boniface Down—came under attack. The WAAF radar operators saw squadrons of planes gathering in the channel and contacted RAF Fighter Command. Fighters took to the air to meet the oncoming bombers. Unfortunately, the radar operators did not see the Stuka dive bombers approaching from inland. Fifteen JU-88 Stuka dive bombers peeled away from a squadron attacking Portsmouth and headed for the radar station.

Coming in on a shallow dive, they dropped four 250-kilogram delayed action bombs. A horrified technician repairing one of the radar masts saw the bombers coming, but did not have time to get down before the attack began. With bombs falling and bullets flying, he made it to the shelter in double quick time. Three WAAFs (a radar operator and two telephone operators) stayed at their posts throughout the raid. They received commendations for their bravery and ten days "survivor leave."

When the bombs exploded, a pall of white and black smoke went up above the inferno that destroyed the buildings. A second attack by another six planes put the station out of operation for two months. However, within three days, a mobile unit at nearby Bembridge continued surveillance until the more sophisticated center was rebuilt.

In early August, Goering ordered massive attacks on airfields to destroy the planes on the ground. Waves of bombers at high and low levels attacked several different targets at the same time. Low level Dornier bombers succeeded in evading radar, and sometimes, the first warning fighter pilots had were bombs falling on their airfield. Dodging the bomb craters, they still managed to take to the air, but more and more fields were destroyed.

With the concentrated attacks on airfields, ports, and shipping, the fighters needed to be nearer the coast to engage the Luftwaffe before they hit their targets. Fighter Command set up satellite airfields on the coast. Fortunately, Spitfires and Hurricanes could take off on grass, so small civilian fields were utilized. In some cases, the airfields were no more than a farmer's fields with a hedge or two removed. Due to the primitive accommodation, squadrons took turns in manning temporary airfields.

Later the temporary airfields became more sophisticated. Level land was plowed, and concrete poured to create an airstrip. Anderson huts were put in place, and communication and servicing equipment moved in. Another airfield was in business.

However, ground crews having to service widely dispersed squadrons were stretched to the limit. Relentless pressure meant being in readiness from 3.30 a.m. to 11.30 p.m. Many went for days without seeing their bunk, and exhausted crews were often found sound asleep on the grass as the squadron took off. In the desperate attempt to keep planes in the air, they continued to work during air raids. The casualties mounted.

In one case, a squadron of hurricanes returning to a bombed airfield near the South Coast asked for permission to land. Directed to another field, the squadron leader said, "We can't make it. We're out of fuel."

A sigh. "Oh well, okay, but remember to dodge the bomb craters."

That night, civilian engineers started up the emergency generators. The army moved in, filled in the craters, and dealt with some unexploded bombs. By first light, the airfield was back in operation.

Fortunately, the exhausted pilots retained their sense of humor. One airborne pilot, asked for assistance by another fighter, answered, "Sorry, old boy, I've got three ME 109s on me. Don't worry though, I've got them surrounded."

It seemed the mighty Luftwaffe could not beat their determined rivals. The Spitfire was a far lighter and more maneuverable plane than the Messerschmitt. Furious with Goering's failure, Hitler asked why, when he had been given everything he asked for, he could not defeat the tiny RAF. Goering replied, "Well, with a squadron of Spitfires, I could." However, no matter how many planes the RAF brought down, numbers were on the side of the Luftwaffe. Britain was short of pilots and short of planes.

The Spitfire Fund was set up to raise money for more planes, and across the country, fund raising campaigns were underway. If any town, or in our case, the Island, could raise £6,000 towards the £11,000 needed to produce a Spitfire, then the Ministry would supply the rest. People everywhere donated savings, spare cash, items for auction and children gave their pocket money.

Some people donated substantial sums, large companies raised money internally, but everyone helped. The Island's total crept up little by little as each town and village contributed. The efforts under way were published each week in the local newspaper.

For example:
- a cricket match on the green at St. Helens raised £1.2s.
- the Girl Guides subscribed £3
- a dance in the Legion Hall raised £8.5s.
- the Women's Institute's bring-and-buy sale raised £8

- a concert given in their backyard by four Cowes schoolgirls raised £1.4s.
- an exhibition of a crashed Messerschmitt at the fire station raised £360.

The fire service had moved a crashed Messerschmitt to their headquarters and charged the public sixpence to sit in the cockpit. An enterprising local printer made a number of mock In Memoriam cards, which sold for three pence and added to the fund.

In joyful remembrance of the fate of the
MESSERSCHMITT 109 one of
HITLER'S NAZI CIRCUS which finished its aerial career at
Bathingbourne Farm, on Friday, August 16
1940
—

May its end be followed by many others.

In the Battle of Britain, which was the first battle in history to be decided purely in the air, the RAF did at least have home advantage. German pilots shot down were taken prisoners, whereas RAF pilots frequently parachuted to safety, caught a train back to base, and were up in the air and fighting again the same day.

Not that German pilots parachuting into England were ill-treated. I overheard my father say to a friend, "A German pilot bailed out over the downs on Tuesday. Large as life, he walked to the nearest road and flagged down a lorry. The driver took him to a pub and called the police." He laughed. "While they waited, the landlord gave the pilot a pint."

"Same as that one those farmhands arrested last week. When they turned him over to the special constable, he marched him to the pub, called into headquarters, then shared a drink with him until the officers arrived!"

Throughout the battle, while the fighters defended Britain, bomber command flew nonstop sorties over France, destroying a good percentage of the invasion barges waiting to launch Operation Sea Lion.

However, in spite of the numbers shot down, the bombers kept coming, and the Luftwaffe still outnumbered the RAF. They could afford to lose planes. The RAF could not. In a war of attrition, the Luftwaffe must win.

Fighter pilots, robbed of sleep, constantly scrambling to fight another wave of bombers, grew raw-nerved and exhausted. Ground crews were stretched well beyond their limits. The Luftwaffe started night raids to prevent airfields from being repaired overnight. With the number of RAF pilots and planes dwindling, the situation grew critical. How much longer could they keep it up?

Then fate and Churchill intervened.

Chapter Twelve

When a disoriented Luftwaffe pilot bombed London, Churchill reacted immediately. If the Nazis intended to wage war on civilians, then Berlin must suffer the consequences. The next night, eighty one RAF bombers attacked Berlin.

Goering suffered deep humiliation, having boasted that no bomb would ever fall on German soil. Hitler, outraged by this assault on the German capital, declared that if Churchill dared to bomb Berlin, he would "bury" London. Churchill had managed to hit Hitler in his most vulnerable spot: his ego. The effect was to be disastrous for the civilian population of London, but proved to be a godsend for the beleaguered RAF and a major strategic error on Hitler's part.

On the afternoon of September 7, 1940, an RAF plane patrolling the South Coast of England sighted German aircraft stretching across the horizon. Reporting the approach of enemy aircraft, he was asked, "How many?"

"How many! It's the whole bloody Luftwaffe."

At four o'clock on that sunny afternoon, Londoners looked up in sheer astonishment at the mass of planes approaching. Three hundred and forty eight bombers, escorted by 617 fighters blackened the skies above the capital. Sirens wailed, as wave after wave of twenty to thirty bombers came in at different heights from different angles. They dropped over three hundred tons of high explosives and hundreds of incendiary bombs. The raid lasted for two hours.

The bombs rained down on the factories and warehouses at London docks and on the surrounding houses. Greater London, with its abundant number of parks, open space and water, is one of the world's least densely populated major cities. However, in 1940, the East End consisted of tightly packed rows of cheaply built homes which housed the dock workers and the businesses serving their needs.

Complete rows of houses collapsed as the bombs struck. The contents of warehouses went up in flames. As barrels of peppercorn caught fire and exploded, they loaded the air with stinging particles. Blazing rivers of rum flooded the streets. A paint fire cascaded white hot flame, a rubber fire spewed thick black smoke, and timber burned fiercely. Flames leapt from building to building, turning the whole area into a raging inferno.

As the incendiary bombs fell in clusters and ignited in a fierce white light, wardens rushed to douse them with sand. Fire engines raced to the scene, but no sooner did they get a fire under control than more bombs dropped, igniting the area again. The air filled with a dark pall of smoke. A cacophony of throbbing bomber engines, screeching fighters, bombs exploding, and buildings crashing down deafened the firemen and wardens. The shouts of wardens, the pulse of pumps, and the hiss of steam added to the chaos.

The fire brigades, with seventy percent new recruits having little or no experience, fought ceaselessly against the inferno. Choking on fumes and suffering burns to their eyes, most had to work forty straight hours. All the reserves were in action.

Ambulance crews, dodging falling bombs and craters, sped to the aid of victims trapped in their demolished houses. Picking their way through streets blocked by piles of rubble, craters, and the snaking coils of fire hoses, many crews simply abandoned their ambulances and ran into the smoke with stretchers.

At six in the evening, the Luftwaffe returned to France, only to be replaced two hours later by more bombers guided in by the light of fires set by the first assault. The second group continued bombing until four thirty the next morning. The London Blitz had begun.

The Blitz was to continue for another fifty-seven days during which London endured raids by day and night. During each raid, one hundred to two hundred bombers dropped two hundred tons of high explosives and three hundred incendiary bombs. Sometimes, twice that many carried out the assault. Bombers swept through in waves, deliberately prolonging the attack to break civilian morale.

For the first few days, the raids continued night and day, but after suffering heavy daytime losses, the Luftwaffe reverted to night time only. The anti-aircraft guns blasted away but with little effect, and the RAF had few night fighters. The scourge of the Luftwaffe, the Hurricanes and Spitfires, lacking radar, could not navigate at night.

On that first night, the blaze as the sun sank was visible all over London, and people in the West of London stood on rooftops, watching in horror the landscape laid out before them. Fires raged across the entire horizon. Before their eyes, small fires turned into infernos belching black smoke. First, the sinking sun turned the sky, smoke and barrage balloons pink, and as night fell, the East End glowed a fiery orange.

In this night of carnage, over one thousand people were killed and one thousand five hundred seriously injured. The bombs demolished churches, pubs, shops, and rows of houses. Entire rows lost their roofs, and bombs sliced some houses in half. Where houses stood the day before, nothing but bricks, concrete, and matchwood remained.

As the smoke cleared after one explosion, firemen stopped, astounded to see a man balanced on a tiny ledge in his bathroom. The whole house had been sliced in half, and somehow, he had managed to escape death by pressing himself against the tiled wall. In another house, a young woman was found under an upturned bath tub. Stark-naked, she was more embarrassed than frightened. A school, used as a temporary shelter for people who had lost their homes, received a direct hit, killing four hundred people.

Air raid wardens had been recruited to patrol rooftops and extinguish incendiary bombs. Mostly volunteers, they did a full day's work before going on duty. Previously untested, on September 7 they did an incredible job of organizing the evacuation of people from bombed buildings, finding buried people, and calling emergency services. Photos of the Blitz show women wardens still finding time to cuddle frightened children saved from a wrecked house.

The anti-aircraft guns, with newly trained crews and limited range, seemed ineffective against the bombers, and people huddled in their shelters muttered about the lack of resistance. General Frederick Pile, commander of the artillery, came up with an inspired idea. He instructed the gun crews to constantly blast away at the planes regardless of their accuracy. It had the desired effect. Gun barrels ran red hot as the gunners flung themselves into the task, and civilians reassured by the sound of guns striking back at the enemy found it easier to sleep. With the frightening throb of plane engines, whistle of bombs, and massive explosions blocked by the sharp cracking sound of the artillery, they relaxed. Luftwaffe pilots, wary of a sky yellow with bursting shells, flew higher and their accuracy suffered.

Women in the ATS, the Auxiliary Territorial Service—the women's branch of the army—were mostly utilized as drivers or canteen workers. However, they were assigned to anti-aircraft gun crews where they carried out all the duties performed by the men of the Royal Artillery. However, Churchill, hearing of this, was appalled. He believed women would never be able to shoot at a young German pilot, so they were allowed to do everything except aim and shoot. Churchill, in spite of all his prodigious talents and the ability to inspire a nation, clearly did not have a clue about women!

Hitler intended to break the morale of the British people. He believed that faced with such devastation, eight million Londoners would scream at their government to request an armistice. He vastly underestimated the strength of character of his opponents.

Civilians, enraged with the mindless slaughter, became far more determined to defeat him. People who had no sleep, or at best a few hours, turned up for work every morning. By doing war work, they felt they were striking back at a personal enemy. For example, a man coming out from an air raid shelter to find his home a pile of rubble shook his fist at the sky and said, "If you think you're going to stop me going to work, Mr. Hitler, you're dead wrong." He then went straight to his job in a munitions factory. Incredibly, absenteeism from work dropped dramatically.

Another intent of the air raids was to break down the infrastructure of the city in order to dishearten the population. Roads and railways were destroyed. Gas, water, and sewer pipelines were severed. Telephone lines were cut. Repairs became top priority, and people worked with dedication during the raids to repair damage in record time.

The city continued to function. In spite of the onslaught on the dockland warehouses, the Port of London continued to operate throughout WWII and was, as always, the busiest port in the country.

On the morning after the first raid, people went to work as usual, buses ran, and couples strolled arm in arm down Piccadilly. Throughout the Blitz, people continued their everyday lives. They went to work, shopped, and visited restaurants, cinemas, and theaters. If a theater was bombed, the actors would find a building elsewhere and put on the play. The Windmill, a show with lots of leggy young women and a few nudes, remained open every night and adopted the slogan "We Never Closed."

Bombs fell on the BBC, and as Bruce Belfrage read the nightly news, an unexploded bomb detonated, killing seven people. Covered in plaster from the ceiling, and his face blackened by smoke, he continued to read without a single tremor in his voice.

London hotel restaurants and cabarets continued to thrive. The Savoy, being blessed with an underground banqueting area, turned one half into a restaurant and night club and the other half into a dormitory shelter for their clients. When a raid started, staff converted the restaurant area to a dormitory.

People adjusted to sleeping in shelters. Each evening, when the air raid siren went, they picked up their cushions, blankets, thermos flasks, and knitting and set off for the shelter. Settling down in their customary places, they chatted to their neighbor for a while and then read, knitted, did crosswords, or played cards. Parents read bedtime stories to children and tucked them up for the night under a blanket, on a bench, or on the floor.

Each morning, even after the most devastating raids, the birds perched on burnt out buildings or blackened trees and sang. They never deserted London throughout its trials.

Cats and dogs suffered with their owners. However, some became heroes. A scruffy stray terrier slunk up to an air raid warden's post. A warden took pity on the dog and took him home. "Rip" soon became the team's mascot and unofficial search dog. Untrained, he instinctively began digging, pausing to let his owner know when he located a victim in the rubble. During heavy gunfire and bombing raids, he remained on duty, never getting in the way but working quickly to find casualties. Over one hundred people owed their life to Rip, and he was awarded the PDSA (the People's Dispensary for Sick Animals) Dickin medal—the equivalent of the Victoria Cross. In April 2009, his medal sold at auction for a record £24,500. Rip, an old dog, died in 1946.

In 1939, animals at the London Zoo were moved to the safety of a country zoo. However, in 1941, authorities decided to open the London Zoo in keeping with other places of entertainment. The animals returned, and the zoo, located in the comparative safety of Regent's Park, did not suffer any raids.

In Belfast, lions, tigers, bears, and wolves were put down in case they ran loose during a raid. However, a kind-hearted elderly lady adopted a baby elephant called Sheila and kept her in her back garden for several months until the raids were over. Sheila survived the war.

The London Underground became an impromptu shelter for as many as 177,000 people at night. They slept on the platforms, lying fully dressed under blankets. The sleepers left just enough room on the platform for the early travelers to catch their trains. As the war progressed, bunks were installed. However, only four percent of the population took advantage of this shelter, sixty percent stayed in their homes, and the rest moved into garden Anderson shelters or public shelters.

King George VI and Queen Elizabeth, parents of the present Queen Elizabeth, visited the East End regularly and commiserated with the bewildered, bombed-out residents. She, immaculate in hat, coat, and the inevitable strings of pearls, and the King, in naval dress uniform.

Buckingham Palace was bombed three times. On the first occasion, the Queen, on inspecting the damage next day, said, "Thank goodness we've been bombed at last. Now, I can look the East Enders in the face."

During another attack, the royal couple sat watching a bomber approach and drop a bomb only eighty yards from their window. Fortunately, the casement window was open or they would have been severely injured by flying glass. They escaped injury. After the attack, a Spitfire pounced on the hapless bomber, and a crowd standing in the Mall cheered the Spitfire on as if they were at a football match. The bomber was shot down.

On another occasion, a Hurricane pilot saw another bomber approaching the palace, and out of ammunition, rammed it. Both planes crashed. Neither pilot was killed, and in fact, the Hurricane pilot lived to the ripe old age of ninety-one. No doubt repeating his story with gusto many times.

Outnumbered and handicapped at night, the RAF did everything in its power to break up the attacks, and shot down bombers as they returned home at daybreak. They even used obsolete bombers to create a screen over the Channel. The RAF bombers climbed high above the oncoming bombers and as the Luftwaffe approached the British coast, sea mines, fitted with parachutes and cables, were dropped in their path. If a Luftwaffe plane hit a cable, it wrapped around the plane and the mine exploded!

City dwellers are seldom friendly with their neighbors and at best mutter a terse good morning or a brief word about the weather. But during the Blitz, people became extraordinarily friendly. The wardens, the ARP, first-aid workers, canteen staff, and the person next to them in the shelter all lived within the same few hundred yards of brick and stone. They suddenly had a great deal in common. Sitting side by side in shelters, they swapped war stories and helped each other out.

People helped however they could. When the gas lines were cut, those with electric stoves shared their cookers with people who had gas. Strangers shared scarce taxis, and restaurant customers often invited people to stay in their home or shelter if the air raid siren sounded when the others were far from home. Streets organized firefighting parties to defend their neighborhood and to repair each other's houses. If a "regular" elderly couple was missing from a shelter, two or three people left the safety of the shelter and ran around to their house to see if they needed help. After a raid, people stood gossiping with their neighbors or went to the pub on the corner for a fortifying beverage.

The government offered my aunt and uncle a condominium in a delightful area in Southern England when their house was bombed. As they said goodbye to their elderly neighbor who had also lost her house, she appeared frightened. On discovering that she feared moving to a new area full of strangers, they took her along with them. She lived with them until her death in 1950.

Whereas elderly people suffered the disruption to their lives during the raids, the young enjoyed the excitement, and everyone felt exceptionally alive. Everyone, young and old, was eager to have fun at dances, pubs, and parties.

On September 12, a bomb fell close to St. Paul's Cathedral and buried itself beneath the roadway next to the southwest tower. Had the eight-foot-long bomb, weighing a ton, exploded, it would have ruined Wren's masterpiece. The roads around the Cathedral were immediately sealed by the police and, for the first and only time during the war, the Cathedral closed. Extracting the bomb became a perilous task. It fell at an angle and continued to sink slowly in the clay. A small party of engineers, led by a Canadian, Lieutenant Davies, began to dig it out. As it slid, it severed a gas main, and fumes overcame several of the engineers before igniting. Fears that the fire would ignite the bomb did not deter gas emergency workers from quelling the flames. Lieutenant Davies continued to work on the slippery bomb and finally managed to extract it. He then had it loaded on a truck and drove through London at extreme speed. When exploded on Hackney Marshes, the bomb created a hundred-foot-wide crater.

The second incident involving the Cathedral drew worldwide attention. On a Sunday evening at the end of Christmas week, a firestorm engulfed the City of London, home of the financial district, Fleet Street, St. Paul's Cathedral, and many famous old buildings dating back to the seventeenth century.

Over six hundred canisters of incendiaries were dropped to disastrous effect. A fifty-mile-per-hour westerly wind fanned the flames, and bombs severed the water main, causing the water pressure to drop dramatically. Frustrated firemen stood holding hoses which merely trickled water. The Thames, at an abnormally low ebb, was out of reach of the emergency pumps installed on the embankment and bridges. Fireboats were immobilized downstream of Tower Bridge by an unexploded parachute mine.

Parachute mines were, in fact, sea mines fitted with a parachute, and the monsters, weighing over a ton, floated silently down. An unnerving sight. The noise of the explosion, unmuffled by earth, was deafening.

The raid was a short one, lasting only two hours. However, when it ended, 1,400 fires burned in the City. These joined to form two huge conflagrations, one over a quarter of a mile long, which consumed everything in their path. For miles around, the sky was bright orange-red.

As several buildings burned to the ground, people in the shelters beneath the buildings were evacuated to the Underground on the other side of the street. They braved sparks driven down the street by the high wind like a blizzard of red hot snow, as around them bombs crashed, buildings collapsed with dull thuds, and the fire roared. In the safety of the Underground, wardens gave the survivors hot tea and wrapped them in blankets.

The fire destroyed eight classic eighteenth century Wren churches and damaged the Guildhall. In the middle of the walls of flame and billowing smoke, St. Paul's Cathedral stood, magnificently firm, untouched in the very center of the destruction.

During the raid, over twenty incendiaries landed on St. Paul's. A few bounced off the Dome, but many more reached the dry, ancient beams. The men of St. Paul's Cathedral Watch—clerics, laymen attached to the chapter, and volunteers, among them many architects—fought the fires.

People standing on rooftops all over London watched the incredible scene. Flames engulfed the whole horizon, turned clouds of billowing smoke red, and illuminated barrage balloons in eerie daylight. Suddenly, the smoke parted, and St. Paul's emerged unscathed, its huge dome standing majestically above the conflagration. They stood awestruck at the seeming miracle.

Perhaps it is best seen through the eyes of an East Ender: "I went up to the roof with some of the firemen to look at the City . . . I could see St. Paul's standing there and fire all around it. And I said, 'Please God, don't let it go!' I was crying, I couldn't help it. I felt that if it went, somehow London would never be the same. But it stood in defiance, it did. And when the boys came back, the firemen said, 'It's bad, but the old church stood it.' Lovely, that was."

It became a symbol of the hope, resilience, and strength of the city.

*   *   *

On September 15, Goering, determined to finish off his tiresome opponent, ordered another all-out assault on London. The intelligence reports he received said the RAF was down to the last few planes, tired, and disorganized.

The brave young German pilots who had been flying nonstop for months did not share this view. They found the persistent fighters, and the now-spirited anti-aircraft guns, a constant threat. Tired and discouraged, they doubted a high command that repeatedly told them just one more push, and it would all be over.

On the other hand, the RAF pilots felt fresh and confident. When bombing attacks on their airfields ceased, they had time to rest, and runways and planes were repaired. With new strategies in place, and more new pilots prepared for combat, the RAF was ready and eager to continue the fight.

The fifteenth was a brilliantly clear, sunny day, perfect for flying. Fighter Command knew the bombers would be coming. However, Lieutenant General Kesselring, Luftwaffe Chief-of-Staff, still did not understand the efficiency of the RAF's warning system. When radar operators reported another huge armada of planes assembling over France and crossing the channel, more fighters thundered down the runways of Southern Command than at any other time during the battle. Fighters climbed to between fifteen thousand and twenty-five thousand feet to await the enemy.

When they arrived, the Spitfires attacked the Messerschmitt fighters, while squadrons of Hurricanes waited for the bombers. The lead squadrons used an unusual method—head on in a shallow climb. With total aggression, the rest followed, shooting down many bombers and scattering their formations. Bombers dropped their loads indiscriminately and headed for home. The Messerschmitts, out of fuel, returned to base and left many hapless bombers at the mercy of their attackers. One Hurricane pilot shot down a plane, which exploded so close to him that his plane went into a tailspin. He bailed out and landed on the sloping roof of a house in London, slid down, and ended up in a garbage bin.

The exhausted RAF pilots—gulping down mugs of strong tea while the ground crews refueled and re-armed their planes—knew the enemy would be back. Once again, swarms of Dorniers and Heinkels formed over the South Coast, but this time, they circled, waiting for their Messerschmitt escort. The fighters climbed, ready to attack again. The fight between the RAF fighters and Messerschmitts was fierce. However, when the Messerschmitts ran out of fuel and returned to base, the bombers were left exposed. Few bombers made it to the intended target, and those that escaped the fighters jettisoned their bombs on the unfortunate population of the London suburbs and headed for home.

The RAF had won a decisive victory. Two days later, realizing the RAF could not be defeated, Hitler called off Operation Sea Lion. Britain would not be invaded. Hitler had been handed his first defeat since 1939.

The Battle of Britain was the first battle ever decided solely in the air. Churchill summed up the RAF's valor by saying "Never in the field of human conflict was so much owed by so many to so few."

The Blitz, during which a million houses were destroyed or damaged, ended in May 1941. Bombing of Britain would continue for several years but never again with such intensity.

Chapter Thirteen

*J*ust two weeks after the *Volendam* left Liverpool, another ship set out for Canada, carrying more CORB children.

The *SS City of Benares* joined convoy OB 213 on Friday, September 13. On board were ninety children under the CORB evacuation scheme, with eight escorts, a doctor, and a nurse. Among the passengers were two girls who had been rescued from the *Volendam* and one of the *Volendam* escorts, a Canadian RCMP. As flagship of the convoy of nineteen ships, the liner carried the convoy Commodore, Rear Admiral Mackinnon, RNR and his staff.

The *City of Benares*, a new ship, pride of the City Line, weighing 11,081 tons, was built for the India run. Captained by Landles Nicholl, she had British officers and a new Lascar (Indian) crew.

For five days, the children, oblivious to danger, played games and had fun on the luxurious liner. The escorts and other passengers felt tense as the convoy zigzagged its way past mines and U-boats. However, five days out from Liverpool they relaxed, knowing they were now beyond the reach of submarines. At this point, the escorting destroyer and two sloops left convoy OB 213 to meet and escort a convoy from Halifax back to Liverpool. The shortage of escort vessels at this stage of the war necessitated leaving a convoy once it was five days out to shepherd an incoming convoy through the danger zone.

Admiralty standing orders stated that convoys should scatter when they no longer had an escort and make for port with all speed. All the larger ships could outrun U-boats, and the smaller ones, once scattered, presented a less inviting target. For some unknown reason, the commodore did not give the command, and the omission proved fatal.

That night, the winds freshened to force six, intermixed with huge wind gusts and icy showers of hail. Battling against the wind and heavy seas, the ship's speed was reduced to six and a half knots. A perfect target for Kapitänleutnant Heinrich Bleichrodt commanding U-48 stalking the convoy at periscope depth.

The children went to bed at 7.30 p.m., and the escorts sat over a drink in the lounge, fully believing they were out of danger. At ten o'clock, U-48 launched one five-hundred-pound torpedo, sufficient to send the *City of Benares* to the bottom of the ocean in thirty minutes.

The torpedo struck amidships, creating a massive hole just below the area where the children slept. Thirty of the children were killed instantly by the force of the explosion. The rest were thrown from their bunks. The engine room flooded, the ship listed to port and started to sink by the stern. Captain Nicholl sounded the "Abandon Ship" alarm.

The lights failed temporarily. In the confusion, the children fumbled their way out to the fume-filled gangways, putting on life jackets but no warm clothing. Their overcoats, set at the foot of the bed with their life jackets the night before, were neglected in the hurry to escape from the cabin.

Escorts rushing to their aid found their way blocked by debris. Together with the ship's officers, they cleared the way, tearing down shattered partitions with their bare hands. Many sustained injuries in their frantic haste to save the children.

The escorts hustled the children to the lifeboats and loaded them in. As the ship started to founder, lifeboats were launched. However, in contrast to the smooth, efficient operation on the *Volendam*, the disaster was exacerbated by the hasty launching into mountainous seas as the ship sank.

The bow of the first lifeboat hit the water before the stern line could be cut. As the crew started to cut it, a huge wave slammed into the boat, throwing the children into the sea. Having survived the explosion, they had little chance of survival in the icy ocean.

In the second lifeboat, the bow dropped with a violent jerk, leaving the stern tilted to an impossible angle. The passengers clung on like monkeys to avoid being spilled overboard.

In the panic as the ship slipped lower and lower into the water, boats were lowered half full. Passengers climbed down ropes and jumped aboard. Few made it as the massive waves tossed the lifeboats around like corks. Passengers threw life rafts over the side and jumped in after them. As the boat sank, one boy incredibly waited for a wave to pick a lifeboat up level with the ship and then jumped into the boat.

Towering waves broke over the successfully launched lifeboats, filling them to the gunnels, forcing passengers to sit waist-deep in icy water.

Seamen pulled frantically on the oars to avoid the ship's fierce undertow as she went down. One lifeboat pulled away with such speed that it became detached from the rest and found itself alone on the black ocean. Six hundred miles from the nearest land.

The two ships on either side of the *City of Benares*, ordered to pick up survivors should she be hit, were both torpedoed. The rest of the convoy, obeying the rules of convoy, scattered, leaving the *City of Benares* to its fate. The survivors were on their own in the middle of an Atlantic gale in open boats.

The *City of Benares* sent out an SOS as she went down, but unfortunately no ships were anywhere near. The closest, *HMS Hurricane*, a naval destroyer escorting another convoy, responded. But, hampered by heavy seas and gale force winds, it took over twenty hours before it reached the survivors. The gale continued to whip up huge breaking seas, and icy showers pelted down on the survivors huddling in the lifeboats. Sitting in icy water, in a freezing wind and sleet showers, the small children dressed in nothing but their nightclothes and lifejackets had little chance of survival. An escort wrote later: " . . . the little ones faded out, quite unable to stand up to the terrible conditions . . . all we could do was hold them above the water until they were gone."

In another lifeboat, an adult recalled: " . . . the children started to go into a coma one by one. We did everything we could, but it was no use."

A dying woman asked someone to hold her hand, and an eleven-year-old boy rushed to her aid. He cradled her head on his knee, stroked her hair, and told her rescue was on the way. A man who witnessed the scene recalled: " . . . . that boy's courage gave me the will to go on."

In the middle of the stormy night, the occupants of one lifeboat heard singing from across the crashing waves. They followed the sound to find two CORB girls, Beth Cummings, fourteen, and Liz Walder, fifteen, clinging to the keel of an upturned lifeboat, singing as if they were on an outing. They were dragged aboard and happily survived. On reaching land, when interviewed by reporters, Beth said, "I had never swum before that night. But I swam to a lifeboat. I don't know how I did it, but I did."

Clinging to the upturned lifeboat with the two girls was a seaman. "He was in terrible shape," Beth said. "But we kept telling him to hang on, and we were very relieved when someone picked us up."

When *HMS Hurricane* found the wreckage and the lifeboats, the crew was appalled and angered by the scene. Lifeboats full of passengers with few survivors. Some even without a single survivor.

One hundred and five cold-numbed and salt-encrusted survivors were taken aboard and given warm clothes and bunks by the crew. All but three survived. The three children were buried at sea with full naval honors.

Parents of the children received a letter from the CORB headquarters: "I am distressed to inform you that, in spite of all the precautions taken, the ship carrying your child to Canada was torpedoed on Tuesday night, 17 September. I am afraid your child is not among those reported as rescued, and I am informed there is no chance of there being any further list of survivors . . ."

One family of ten children lost five children in the disaster. Ironically, the five who remained in London survived an air raid that destroyed their house. The father, incensed and well over the age of conscription, immediately joined the army, vowing "to get that Hitler."

Of the ninety children aboard *SS City of Benares*, there were apparently only seven survivors. However, the lifeboat separated by the storm had another six boys on board and with them was an escort, Mary Cornish, a single, forty-one-year-old Londoner. Mary had studied music in Vienna and London and taught music privately. After having torn away the debris to free her charges, she returned below to rescue more children. An officer ordered her to go to the lifeboats since he had already checked and the ship was sinking fast.

When she arrived on deck, her children had left, so she was loaded into a lifeboat containing six little boys. The boat was thirty feet long and crammed with forty-six people: thirty-two Indian seamen, the boys' male escort (a Roman Catholic priest), the ship's fourth officer, a signalman, a steward, a stoker, a Polish passenger, Mary Cornish, and six boys. They also found a cadet in the water totally spent after diving repeatedly to save other passengers. He was hauled aboard in a state of total exhaustion, but, as an amateur yachtsman, proved to be a valuable asset. The occupants of the lifeboat were packed so tightly together they could not move without treading on other people.

The occupants of the lifeboat watched, transfixed, as the *City of Benares*, all lights blazing, dipped her bow, reared her stern, and like a sea monster, slipped beneath the waves. They were plunged into darkness, surrounded by black mountainous waves. Pieces of wreckage and an empty lifeboat drifted by. To those in the boat, it seemed as if hours had gone by since the torpedo struck, but it was only thirty minutes.

All night long, the wind screamed around them, and the waves pounded the side of the boat. The fourth officer, on the tiller, ordered everyone to take a turn propelling the boat forward to keep the head into the wind to prevent the boat from capsizing. The priest took one turn, but then, completely incapacitated by seasickness, lay on the bottom of the boat.

The lifeboat, a clinker-built boat, was open to the elements, equipped with one small sail and a propelling apparatus operated by five sets of two handles set on the bottom of the boat between the seats. Unfortunately, the elongated handles, similar to those used to draw beer, dug in the back of the nearest passenger whenever they were operated. During the night, the steward served a drop of brandy all round.

Finally, the freezing, interminable night ended, and a gray dawn broke. They looked around them. No rescuing ship rushing to their aid. No other lifeboats. Nothing but pieces of wreckage bobbing by. The wind continued to rise, whipping the huge waves into a frenzy.

With daylight, the steward, who had reassured the passengers during the night, set about making them as comfortable as possible.

The lifeboat had shipped water so the combination of feet in icy water and sleet showers propelled by gale force winds made cold the overwhelming enemy. The steward reorganized the seating and issued blankets. The boys, their escorting priest, and Mary Cornish were moved into the bow and the steward rigged a canvas awning to provide some shelter. A locker occupied most of the space in the bow, so the boys arranged themselves on top and around it. The two handles in the bow were taken out of their sockets to make more room. The two escorts, six boys, and later, the Polish passenger, shared a space of about eight by six feet.

Only one of the children had a coat, two wore shoes, and all were in their pajamas. They had two blankets, supplemented by the priest's overcoat, between them. Mary Cornish wore a silk blouse, short-sleeved jacket, and thin skirt.

Lifeboats are stocked with three weeks' supply of food and one week of water. The steward, who was in charge of the provisions, well aware of the shortage of water, gave everyone only one dipper full of water per day. A dipper held less than a quarter of a pint. Thirst from the first day was a severe problem.

After a day totally alone on the vast, heaving ocean, the fourth officer, a young man of twenty-two, realized there was little hope of rescue. Refusing to give up hope, he set a course eastward toward the nearest land, Ireland. Heading toward land and the shipping lanes, they might see another ship.

As the gale continued to rise, he called for volunteers to man the four pairs of handles. On the second day, when the wind at last abated, the cadet hoisted the sail. Everyone cheered up as they whipped along toward the coast. The steward served a meal at noon: one sardine each on a ship's biscuit and a dipper of water. Everyone wanted more water, but he rationed it rigorously, knowing that it would have to last a long time.

For the first two days, the boys, whose ages ranged from eight to thirteen, were lively and cheerful in spite of the cold and the pitching boat. It was a great adventure, and they were sure a destroyer would be along to pick them up. Hungry, they fantasized about the meals they would eat when they arrived back on land. They argued about which would be best but generally settled on their favorite—fish and chips. Mary Cornish had them singing songs, and their high voices rose above the storm as they bellowed *Run rabbit, run rabbit, run, run, run.*

As the days wore on, hunger died as the pangs of thirst tormented them. Throats swelled, and tongues became too encrusted with salt to sing. The children tried to eat the bully beef or sardine issued to them, but none could eat the dry biscuits.

The weather continued gray and cold. Life in the boat was a continual battle to stave off the effects of the cold and thirst. As the interminable days wore on, Mary Cornish realized she had to keep the boys' minds off the misery of cold, hunger, and thirst, so she told them to watch for ships by day and made up a Bulldog Drummond story every night.

The days crawled by without the sight of a ship. They tried to keep clean by dangling a handkerchief over the side of the boat on a string and washing their hands and face. The stoker, in his forties and an experienced seaman, was wiry and tough, and took being shipwrecked in his stride. Once the gale abated, he stripped off his clothes and took a swim each day.

The Lascars were meticulous in keeping clean, washing out their shirts and turbans frequently. As was their custom, they washed out their mouths before praying, using seawater as a substitute for fresh water.

The boys' spirits remained high in the day as they scanned the horizon for rescue ships. Each one took a turn standing up, hanging on to the mast, and scanning the horizon for ships. Their young eyes were sharp and didn't miss a thing, but even they could not conjure up a ship or a plane. Each night, the priest would lead them in the Lord's Prayer, they would say their own prayers then settle down on the hard wood to try and sleep. Sometimes during the night, the misery of the cold, the unbearable thirst, and sheer fright would cause one of them to whimper. Mary Cornish dealt with this by saying brusquely, "Don't you realize that you're the hero of a *real* adventure story? There isn't a boy in England who wouldn't give his eyes to be in your shoes. Did you ever hear of a hero who sniveled?"

It worked every time. The boy's attention was turned from self-pity to the delight of their parents when they returned and the awed admiration of their school friends.

After the first four days, the boys' feet and legs began to give trouble. Without movement, the heart could not pump enough blood to nourish them. The first stages of death from exposure threatened them. Mary Cornish massaged their feet and legs before they went to sleep and again when they woke in the night.

Her own feet felt like blocks of ice. She solved this by volunteering to take a turn working the handles during the night to get her circulation going. The boys took turns at first, but within three days their strength gave out. During the day, she cut buttons from her blouse for the boys to suck to assuage the pangs of thirst.

One boy grew delirious and started screaming in the night. Mary Cornish and the priest did everything in their power to comfort him, but still, the screams for water continued. Worried his screams might cause a panic among the Lascars, Mary gave up her blouse and the cadet his coat to keep the boy warm, and the stoker smuggled an extra dipper of water to him. The Lascars, Muslims, bitterly resented any preferential treatment given to a woman and children. They kept the one flashlight in the boat trained on the boy during the night to make sure their precious water supply was not used on him. Finally, the stoker, a man with a large family, persuaded the boy that rescue would come next day and quieted him down.

The days of misery, punctuated by short bursts of excitement when a cloud on the horizon looked like a ship's smoke, followed by bitter disappointment, continued. On the seventh day, the steward dolled out the usual water ration, but he knew it would have to be halved the next day if they were to survive. On the eighth day, the deep gray of the ocean began to turn to blue-green, a sign of land and shipping lanes. Finally, a boy, wild with excitement, sighted a plane—a Sunderland of Coastal Command on routine patrol. A distress flag, Mary Cornish's petticoat, was hoisted to the masthead, and the plane spotted them. As the Australian pilot flew low over them and waved, the boys managed a cheer from their parched throats.

Soon afterwards, another plane flew over and dropped supplies. The supplies bobbed up and down in the waves, and the boys squealed with excitement as the fourth officer maneuvered the lifeboat close enough to pick up a bundle. The stoker leaned way over and grabbed one. It was passed, hand over hand, to the steward, who set about breaking it open helped enthusiastically by his passengers. Canned peaches, bully beef, and baked beans. He handed out cans of peaches, and everyone sighed in bliss as the sweet liquid trickled down their parched throats.

HMS Anthony, a destroyer, was soon on the scene. Coming alongside and using the ship to shelter the lifeboat from the oncoming waves, seamen threw rope ladders and netting over the side and, beaming from ear to ear, scrambled down and grabbed the boys. Next, Mary Cornish, too weak to move, was picked up by a seaman and carried aboard. All the other passengers followed. The sailors eager for a long, cool drink followed by a tot of rum.

Once on board the destroyer, the boys were given warm water laced with sugar, fed, checked by a doctor, and given a bed. All the destroyer's officers gave up their bunks, and the crew most of their warm clothing. Next morning, as bright as buttons, apparently no worse for their ordeal, the boys turned up in Mary Cornish's cabin wearing huge naval sweaters and long woolen stockings.

Mary Cornish, once on board, too weak to undress, tried to wash and brush her teeth. She remembered looking at them and deciding a chisel would be more appropriate. They were encrusted with salt.

The British public was appalled by the *City of Benares* disaster. Their fury at the targeting of children by the Germans was fueled by emotive articles like this, mildly inaccurate one, in the Daily Mirror:

83 CHILDREN DIE AS HUNS

SINK LINER IN STORM

Eighty-three out of a party of ninety children being taken to Canada died along with 211 other passengers and crew when a British liner was torpedoed and sunk by Huns in an Atlantic storm.

Seven out of nine adults who were escorting the children were also drowned.

A U-boat committed this crime against civilians when the liner was six hundred miles from land. The ship sank in twenty minutes.

Huge seas swamped some of the boats, which the crew managed to launch. In other boats, people sat waist-deep in water and died of exposure.

Many of the children were killed when the torpedo struck the ship.

The disaster was revealed last night when it was stated officially that the number missing was 294.

There were 406 people in the ship, a crew of 215 and 191 passengers. Including the ninety children who were being evacuated by the Overseas Reception Board.

The 112 survivors included thirty-six Lascars.

Two of the children who were drowned were making their second attempt to reach safety in Canada.

They were rescued from the first evacuee liner to be torpedoed—the Volendam. They were still eager to cross the Atlantic and were embarked on the next available ship. This time, they did not escape the Huns.

Apart from those in the party of ninety evacuee children, a number of children traveling privately with their parents are among the missing.

However, the public was inspired by the rescue of another six boys and the heroism of Mary Cornish. She, along with the fourth officer, a young man of twenty-two who steered the lifeboat to safety, and the steward, was presented with a medal by King George VI in a ceremony at Buckingham Palace.

Two hundred eighty-six of the 406 people on board *SS City of Benares* were lost including the captain, commodore, and six of the children's escorts. Of the ninety CORB children on board, only thirteen survived. Sadly, the *Volendam* survivors, the two children, and the RCMP escort were not among them. The government suspended the CORB program for the winter months, but it was never reinstated as the threat of invasion had passed and the Atlantic remained a dangerous zone.

* * *

In spite of the *City of Benares* disaster, CORB remained popular with the press, and consequently, the public continued to support the scheme. With the Blitz beginning and the Battle of Britain still hanging in the balance, positive propaganda was a necessity.

The torpedoing of the *Volendam*, the swift efficient rescue of the children, and the children's bravery was a tremendous source of anti-Nazi propaganda. Headlines decried the dastardly Germans who waged war on innocent children and praised the survivors whose conduct was worthy of Britain's great naval tradition. All over the country, children from the *Volendam* were eager to go again, and their parents supported them. The press even managed to mitigate grief over the *City of Benares* disaster by focusing on the bravery of the survivors.

The public's wrath was directed at Hitler, who created the situation, rather than at CORB.

* * *

I recently learned I had yet another incredible escape. Plans were made to re-embark some children from the *Volendam* on the *City of Benares*.

My family, and all the other children from the Isle of Wight, were part of a group billeted in Glasgow after the torpedoing of the *Volendam*. This group was scheduled to travel to Liverpool to embark on the *City of Benares*. However, fortunately an eight-year-old caught chicken pox. Since all of us had potentially been exposed to the disease, we were sent home. I am still having trouble believing this stroke of luck.

Chapter Fourteen

O ur quiet residential corner of the Island changed into an area bristling with Canadian soldiers, Italian prisoners of war, and convalescing British servicemen.

The Regina regiment was billeted throughout the area, and two large houses belonging to my relatives were requisitioned by the government. One house was empty, and the other was occupied by an elderly aunt and uncle who were perfectly willing to move to a smaller house.

The soldiers immediately began a rigorous training program in preparation for raids on France. In addition to mock battles on the downs, they exercised on our beach and climbed ropes thrown over the low cliff. Clearly out of condition, they struggled to reach the top while we scampered right past them on other ropes. Not a bit abashed, they laughed at our prowess. We enjoyed talking to them and asking them questions about Canada, but they constantly complained about the cold. In geography at school, I learned that Canada is cold and thick with snow in the wintertime. So why did the Island climate, where snow happened at most once a year, bother them? When I visited Canada after the war, I realized that they came from well-heated houses. In 1940, large English country houses lacked double-glazed windows to keep out the drafts, and adequate central heating. We were accustomed to sitting around an open fire, roasting on one side and freezing on the other.

Village dances, which used to be infrequent and poorly attended, took place each week and burst at the seams as the Canadians welcomed a chance to meet the local girls. Girls and women, who had seen no point in going before, since most of the young local men had left to fight in North Africa or at sea, put on their makeup, primped their hair, wore their best dresses, and joined the throng. Even married women who had not seen their husbands for two years went, eager for any entertainment. Everyone shared the same desire, to have a good time and forget the war for a few hours. Needless to say, the village gossips had a field day. Friends visited my mother, and with a wary eye on us, whispered in her ear. They passed on juicy pieces of gossip with horrified expressions and delighted eyes.

Only a quarter of a mile from our house, Italian prisoners, captured by Montgomery's advancing army, filled a disused fort. Dark-eyed and ill-clad in shapeless prison uniforms, they appeared content to be out of the fight. Shortly after their arrival, they began working on local farms. As willing workers, they enjoyed a large measure of freedom and worked side by side with the Women's Land Army to their mutual delight.

The warm waters of the Gulf of Mexico flow across the Atlantic and wash the shores of the Isle of Wight, creating a more benign climate than that of the mainland. The combination of the warmer climate and clean sea air make it a popular place for convalescing invalids. On the bay next to ours, a cliff-top hotel, closed for the duration, was reopened as a convalescent home for servicemen. With large lawns that swept down to the cliff's edge, it afforded a splendid view of the sheltered waters of the Solent. A view that in peacetime was alive with colorful yachts and luxury liners offered only gray ships slipping silently out to sea. On sunny afternoons, the wounded soldiers, sailors, and airmen, all dressed in the same comfortable loose blue suits and white shirts, sat in wheelchairs on the lawn or hobbled painfully along the shingle paths on the arm of crisply dressed nurses.

My life settled down into its familiar pattern. School each day and on Sunday, with a nicely polished face, I walked to Sunday school. There, I learned all about Moses and the burning bush and missionaries, who, braving all ills, saved the natives in Africa. Sometimes, I went to the adult Sunday service. Before the war, the mile-and-a-half walk to church was a leisurely stroll until the church bell rang. Then a rushed quarter of a mile before we dropped panting into our pews just as the organist's pudgy white hands played the first notes. Now, with church bells silenced until they warned of an invasion, we had to leave fifteen minutes early to be sure we arrived on time.

On Saturdays, we bought our comics, the Beano and the Dandy featuring Desperate Dan and Pansy Potter, the Strong Man's Dotter. Afterwards, I went to the morning movies with my friends and raced to get the best seats in the front row. We watched Disney cartoons, the *Lone Ranger*, and everyone's favorite, *Flash Gordon*. The gray men coming out of the cave walls in *Flash Gordon and the Clay Men* frightened me.

Occasionally, I went with my mother and siblings to the adult movies to see the *Pathe News*, a cartoon, and patriotic films like *In Which We Serve*. Mostly though, we saw escapist musicals or comedies through a blue haze of cigarette smoke.

Since TV was not yet available, we sat in a comfortable fireside circle and listened to variety shows, comedies, and dramas on the radio. Nothing is scarier on a dark night in a dimly lit room, with the wind howling outside, than listening to a spooky drama. We all sat transfixed. No amount of special effects on TV can compete with one's imagination.

After the play ended, we had a hot cup of Horlicks and a piece of cake before going to bed. As the embers settled and the dog snored gently, I felt safe curled up in a chair, cradling my cup.

However, I went upstairs to bed wide-eyed, convinced something was lurking in the shadows. Fortunately, I shared a bedroom with my sister so I did not have to be alone at night. I felt sorry for my poor brother, who slept all alone on the third floor. He just grinned and did not seem a bit bothered. In the daytime, he taunted me with the rhyme:

> *As I was going up the stair,*
> *I met a man who wasn't there.*
> *I met him there again today.*
> *I wish, I wish he'd go away.*

Together with my friends, I went on bicycle rides. Pedaling our upright, one-speed bicycles, we ventured to neighboring villages and to cliff tops overlooking the Channel. With little traffic on the roads, we could ride in safety. Every once in a while, a truckload of soldiers would roar by, waving to us. We waved back with an enthusiasm that jeopardized our balance.

On one gray Saturday morning, with a fog obscuring the horizon, we slid down a low cliff to a stony beach on the South side of the Island. A slow, oily swell rolled in and broke on the shore, receding with a rattle of stones and a loud swish. Brown seaweed hung in the waves and lined the beach. Seagulls squawked and fought over scraps of fish. We crunched along, slipping and sliding on the wet stones and gathering pieces of driftwood and shells. Eyes on our feet as we searched for treasures, we did not notice the strange object until we were half way along the beach. It was floating in on the swell, hitting the beach, and then rolling back out as the wave swished back. A minute later, it came in on the next swell. This continued for several minutes. We watched fascinated, walking closer and closer to get a better look. It was a mine. A big circular object with large, protruding metal knobs. We regarded it seriously for a while.

"Those knobs must be the detonators," Robbie said. "I wonder why it isn't exploding as it hits the beach."

No one answered. After a few minutes, Robbie picked up a large stone and threw it at the mine. Nothing happened. We all joined in, happily tossing stones at the mine for several minutes. No explosion occurred. Growing bored with the lack of action, we crunched our way back to the cliff and cycled home.

My parents did not take a daily newspaper. Only the weekly Isle of Wight County Press newspaper was read cover to cover. Full of news about air raid attacks, fund-raising ventures like raffles, jumble sales, and amateur dramatics. Stories too of service men who had been decorated for bravery and obituaries for those who had died in the North African desert or at sea.

By not taking a daily paper, our parents managed to keep the news of the *City of Benares* tragedy from us. However, they announced on the radio news that CORB had been suspended. At the news, my mother's eyes lit up, and she sang as she did the dishes.

Chapter Fifteen

*T*he *City of Benares* tragedy saw the end of the Children's Overseas Reception Board (CORB). Initially suspended for the winter months, when Hitler abandoned his plans for invasion, the evacuation program ended.

CORB was formed in response to overwhelming offers of support from the Dominions. After the fall of France in May 1940, the Australian, New Zealand, Canadian, and South African governments made formal offers of homes for British children for the duration of the war. In response, CORB was formed with Geoffrey Shakespeare, the Under-Secretary for the Dominions, as Chairman. With invasion imminent, speed was essential, and within six weeks of the formation of the committee, the first children sailed from Liverpool.

The committee faced a daunting mission in organizing the evacuation. They needed to select children suitable for evacuation, decide priorities based on immediate danger, find escorts, and organize transport to and accommodation at the port of embarkation.

Perhaps their most difficult task was to find shipping space. With every liner pressed into service to transport troops to the

Middle East and Far East from Britain, and to carry servicemen and women from the Dominions to war zones, shipping space was scarce. Evacuation was not a priority.

Finding escorts was far easier. When a request for escorts went out in Britain, nineteen thousand people volunteered, and from this base, one thousand were selected. Escorts were selected on the basis of their prior experience with children as teachers, tutors, nurses, ministers, or within organizations such as the Boy Scouts and Girl Guides. One member of the committee also insisted on a high level of agility, realizing adventurous children might attack rails and rigging.

Even being torpedoed did not deter the volunteers. After the *Volendam* was torpedoed, CORB asked ex-*Volendam* escorts if they would be willing to go again. Escorts received letters similar to the following:

Dear Miss Smith,

Although your experience in traveling with a party of children was so unfortunate, I am writing to ask whether you would be willing to help us in this way on another occasion. If so, will you please let me know when you will be free and which of the Dominions you would prefer. We will then let you know when your exit permit is renewed.

They responded with enthusiasm. As one woman said, "I was young. It was a great adventure, and I just didn't think about danger."

One surviving escort volunteered and left on the *City of Benares*. Before he left, he gave all the boys in his *Volendam* group a copy of the New Testament. One of them, John Roberts, received a New Testament with the inscription:

> *To John with best wishes for your future and in commemoration of the torpedoing of our liner the VOLENDAM in the Atlantic on the night of Friday, August 30, '40 at 11.12.*

> *'GOD IN HIS GOODNESS PRESERVED US ALL.'*

> *From your affectionate Canadian Sea Escort Mr. W.Bolton, 'Cosy Cot' Simmondley Glossop, Derbyshire.*

Unfortunately, Mr. Bolton did not survive the torpedoing of the *City of Benares*.

Across the Dominions, thousands offered their homes. Reasons for the offer differed, but many did it out of a sense of patriotism. They felt they were thwarting Hitler by whisking children out of harm's way.

The ties between Britain and the Dominions were strong, and when Britain faced invasion, young men from the Dominions volunteered for the forces in order to defend Britain. Their womenfolk felt equally committed and volunteered to look after evacuees as their part of the war effort.

CORB urged parents to find sponsors in the Dominions. These were frequently relatives or friends who willingly offered to take care of a child for the duration of the war. In some cases, it was a friend of a friend. A friend of Alan Corbishley's mother knew the postmistress in a New Forest town who had a cousin in Saskatchewan who was willing to sponsor a British child. Thus, Alan had a sponsor.

For others, it was, "having no children of our own we thought we should care for one or two of the children." Some wanted a young son or daughter to round out their family. For example, a mother on a farm in New Zealand had three boys and wanted a girl. Some even did it out of a sense of civic duty.

CORB worked closely with their counterparts in the Dominions to ensure a smooth transition for the children, and together, they agreed upon the following division of tasks:

—In Britain, CORB identified suitable children, found shipping space, and provided escorts to take the children to the port of embarkation and others to take care of them on board the ship.

—The Dominions found foster homes for those children not traveling to relatives. They also provided escorts from the disembarkation port to their final destinations and organized regular checks to make sure the children were settling happily.

Dominions were often specific in their requests as to the type of children they wished to receive. For example, a member of the New Zealand parliament suggested that the country would prefer children from "a better class of home."

Both CORB and the Dominions' committees agreed that only children from families would be evacuated. No child from any form of orphanage or institution would be included. This was because of a scandal that had rocked Australia when it was discovered that children sent from British orphanages to homes in Australia were being abused.

CORB publicized the scheme in British schools, and parents were given the option of applying. To be selected, children needed a favorable school report and clearance from doctors and dentists.

Local education authorities provided escorts from the children's homes to the port of embarkation. Education authorities at the two departure ports, Liverpool and Glasgow, provided housing. Children slept on cots, or pallets on the floor, in school classrooms, halls, and gyms.

CORB, anticipating problems with children settling down in their new country, issued a set of guidelines for the Dominions. As the Chairman of CORB stated, "we need to be sure of the most careful arrangements for placing and aftercare . . . and to ensure children are sent to congenial homes." The guidelines suggested:

—prior inspection of all homes
—placement with families from the same social strata
   and religious beliefs
—keeping children of the same family together
 whenever possible or close by
—recognition of friendships formed on the voyage

They also suggested that supervision of evacuees and their foster parents should be left to the local authorities. This caused some problems as each country and local authority differed greatly in its approach. The exception was New Zealand, which kept the supervision centralized under one person in the Welfare Division of the National Government's Education Department. Something feasible in a small, well-organized country like New Zealand.

Care was taken to select suitable foster parents, and letters similar to the one below, mailed in New Zealand, were sent to families who had offered to take a child.

Dear Mr. Jones,

Thank you for your application for two of the children to be evacuated from Great Britain.

My committee has undertaken the responsibility of placing the children in suitable homes. With this end in view, we would like to interview you in your home to establish a friendly contact between the foster parents and the committee.

Would you, therefore, kindly receive two members of the committee in your own home at your convenience. The two members detailed to visit you will ring to make an appointment and will carry with them a letter of introduction.

I trust this arrangement will meet with your approval.

Yours faithfully,

Althea Smith
Secretary

The CORB program captured public imagination on both sides of the Atlantic. People saw the evacuation of children to safety abroad as an act of defiance against Hitler. Its popularity bothered Churchill, who felt evacuation defeatist and lacking the defiant spirit necessary to win a war. His wife, Clementine Churchill, just managed to stop one of their grandchildren leaving on a ship before the news reached Churchill's ears.

Many other children went to the Dominions or the States under private arrangements. A few private schools in England were relocated in their entirety. But very few. This type of evacuation came to a screeching halt when Churchill said it was defeatist.

Queen Elizabeth, the wife of King George VI and mother of the present Queen, did not share his view and sent the following letter to families who hosted CORB children:

I wish to mark, by this personal message, my gratitude for the help and kindness which you have shown to the children who crossed the sea from the United Kingdom many months ago. Since the early days of the War you have opened your doors to strangers and offered to share your home with them. In the kindness of your heart, you have accepted them as members of your own family, and I know that to this unselfish task you and all your household have made many great sacrifices. By your generous sympathy you have earned the true and lasting gratitude of those to whom you have given this hospitality, and by your understanding you have shown how strong is the bond uniting all those who cherish the same ideals.

(signed) Elizabeth

CORB children received rapturous greetings on their way to their destinations. When a ship bound for the Far East and Australia stopped in Cape Town, people rushed down to the docks to take the children on excursions and to entertain them. On hearing from the escorts that CORB had not supplied enough games and books to keep the children occupied during the long weeks of the voyage, they inundated escorts with games and toys.

A liner carrying CORB children, on arrival at the mouth of Sydney harbor in Australia, was greeted by a mass of small boats that accompanied them to their dock. In pulling into dock, the huge bulk of a gray-painted *Queen Mary* loomed over them. She boomed out a welcoming blast on her siren.

Children traveling from Halifax to British Columbia were cheered at every railway station along the way and showered with candies and toys. Most children were bemused by all the attention, but a few loved every moment of it and had a hard time dealing with reality once they reached their destination.

Those children going to relatives, or sponsors, were picked up at the railway station and taken home. Jimmie, a seven-year-old, remembered how nervous he had been about meeting elderly cousins who had agreed to take him.

"I was so nervous, I had to pee three times in the hour I waited at the station. I didn't know these people. What would they be like? Would they like me or be sorry they'd agreed to take me? I wished I was at home."

However, when they arrived, he said, "Wow, she looked exactly like my Gran. I ran right over and hugged her." He spent five happy years with them, and after he returned to England, they visited regularly.

Children without sponsors were taken to holding areas, such as schools or hotels, or in the case of the lucky children going to South Africa, to Westbrooke, the Governor-General's residence in Cape Town. After a health check and inoculations where needed, they were taken to centers where the people, who had volunteered and been prescreened for suitability, came by and selected them.

The youngest children and girls soon found homes, but few people were prepared to take on teenage boys.

Some were lucky enough to be selected by families living a long way out of town who wanted company for their teenage son. Other families, unfortunately, took them because they would be an extra pair of hands on the farm or in the family business. In some cases, the boys were worked so hard their schoolwork suffered, but in most cases, they fitted right in and enjoyed being a useful member of the family. Brian, a fourteen-year-old, said, "The family who fostered me was great. They took me right in. Entertained me, took me on holiday with them, and gave me lots of presents at Christmas. I felt embarrassed sometimes that they were giving me so much."

Families of three or more were generally split up. This, in some cases, proved traumatic for the eldest child who had promised his or her parent to look after the younger ones and keep the family together.

One thirteen-year-old remembered sitting with her fourteen-year-old friend in the center, watching all the young ones being selected and leaving for their new homes. They sat together and waited and waited. The room gradually emptied until they were sitting all alone. Escorts and volunteers fussed around them, but the girls could see from their worried frowns that they were a problem. Their hearts sank. They bit their lips to keep from crying.

Finally, a breathless elderly couple rushed in and said, "Sorry, we're late. Got held up." They looked around and then stared at us. "So, you're all that's left then." We felt horrible and stared at our toes. Then the woman said, her face breaking into a smile, "We'd better be off then." They took us to their car and to the start of "five of the happiest years of our lives."

Local authorities made efforts to match children with the same type of home and people of a similar background, but mismatches occurred. For example, a family of three children was sent to relatives in Australia who were too poor to cope with the additional expense. The children were re-allocated to three separate families. A dock worker's son had difficulty settling in a history professor's home, and a child from a privileged London family and elite school found settling in the Australian outback and cycling to a one-room school with wooden walls and a tin roof "a bit traumatic at first."

Children going to a family with other children generally settled well. The children from the Dominions welcomed the novelty of a kid with a strange accent. Occasional problems arose with jealousy from a spoiled only child. One evacuee remembered on the first day being sent to take a nap with her new "sister" and ending up shut in the wardrobe having to pretend she was a radio.

One foster mother in Canada recalls the problems caused when the neighbors, feeling sorry for the child so far from home, showered attention and parties on him, neglecting her own daughters.

Adult friends of a host family found the CORB children a fascinating diversion and asked them dozens of questions about life in England. The children felt self-important with all the adult questions, but one child wrote to his parents complaining about the endless, repetitive questions. His father wrote back telling him that he must be "patient with these kind-hearted people . . . and remember, you are English and must give them a good impression of English children."

The novelty soon wore off, and the children settled down to life in a different country and culture. Again, the very young ones adapted more easily, simply transferring their affections to their new parents. They missed their mother, and when a woman "mothered" them, they immediately took to her.

The older ones were torn by loyalty to their own parents and felt guilt pangs initially for enjoying life with their foster parents. They were far more self-conscious about their different clothes and accents and tried hard to fit in.

A fourteen-year-old girl remembered feeling lonely and insecure in her new home but said nothing for fear it would upset her parents who were having a bad time during the air raids. She felt awkward among the self-assured young girls in her school, and this was exacerbated by the clothes she wore. Growing quickly, her foster parents, who were pressed for money, obtained clothes for her from the Red Cross. She felt terrible in the less than fashionable clothes but again said nothing. As soon as she could, she left school and enrolled in a business school which offered a year's free tuition for evacuees. With skills, she got a job and started to enjoy life, settling happily. The thoughtfulness of Canadians not directly connected with the resettlement program saved the day.

However hard foster parents worked to keep the children in touch with home, the links weakened as memories faded. Parents wrote regularly from England, but children found it difficult to know what to say in the weekly letters their foster parents insisted they write. Susan remembered the misery of sitting for ages in front of a blank piece of paper trying to think what to say. After the first few letters describing the family and house where she was living, she was stumped. She tried listing the language differences, but that soon ran out. She just couldn't think of a thing. Her parents in war-torn Britain tried to write about anything except the war and shortages for fear of upsetting her. She in turn worried about them and was hungry for news about the situation at home.

A CORB friend told her, "Well, anyway, they can't tell you about the war. My mother tried, but all I got was a letter with blacked out pieces and holes. The censor didn't like it."

Efforts were made to bridge the gap. For example, Canadian cable companies allowed each child to cable monthly without charge. Soon after the children arrived, CORB arranged for photos to be taken and sent home. CORB also arranged with the BBC to have parents talk to their children on the radio. This proved to be a mixed blessing. Host families and the children were wild with excitement, but when the day arrived, the host family sat beaming, knowing the child would be delighted. Whereas the child felt self-conscious under their scrutiny and desperately upset hearing their parents and knowing they could not go to them.

Some children were even embarrassed by the broadcast because their nervous parents standing in a studio with other people felt uncomfortable, and some from poorer homes, even affected a "posh" accent which bewildered their children.

Foster mothers often bridged the gap by writing regularly regarding the child's progress at school and friendships. They appreciated the pain the natural mother must be feeling and endeavored to keep her included in the child's life.

However, no matter how close the ties remained, the children quickly became New Zealanders, Canadian, or Australian. No amount of contact could change that.

Memories of home dimmed. A five-year-old said, "My foster family treated me as one of them, and I loved the life. Memories of home faded, and my real parents became like a favorite auntie and uncle who wrote lots of letters and sent lots of presents." Surrounded by New Zealanders, he became one.

The children were a curiosity at school because of their accents and "strange British clothes." They quickly modified their accents and begged their foster parents for clothes like the other kids. Many children were helped through the adjustment period by other children in their foster family, by neighbor's children, or by "buddies" assigned by teachers. Teachers worked hard to help the children adjust, giving them extra help and turning a blind eye to nervous errors. Most children found that they were well ahead of their peers. Only in New Zealand and South Africa was the curriculum level with the British system.

Adjustments were necessary on both sides. For example, in Canada, foster parents were amazed when British children who were prepared to do chores around the house refused to do a paper route. To a Canadian, a paper route symbolized initiative and responsibility—the qualities needed to succeed in life. In Britain, delivering papers was seen as a badge of poverty and was to be avoided.

Mostly, the children enjoyed the changes particularly, "everything being less formal and children being part of the parent's life instead of being separate."

One man in looking back on his experiences said, tongue-in-cheek, that he thinks he must have been a bit of a handful when he was a kid. His foster parents returned him to the children's organizing committee, saying, "They wanted to do their bit for the war effort, but please, would they take Henry back and find him a new home. They would do *anything* for the war effort except look after him."

As an elderly man, Henry recalled with a laugh, "I think I must have been a holy terror." He settled happily in his new home.

* * *

Before the program ended, CORB had successfully evacuated a total of 2,664 children in just three months:

202 to New Zealand

355 to South Africa

577 to Australia

1,532 to Canada

In addition, 838 went to the United States under the auspices of the U.S. Committee for the Evacuation of European Children with the collaboration of CORB but not under the CORB scheme.

The only casualties were the seventy-three children on board the *City of Benares*. The risks were high at sea but far higher in Britain.

For example, in the month of September 1940, when the *City of Benares* sailed, 6,954 civilians were killed and 10,615 were seriously injured in British cities.

The carnage continued:

—In Coventry on the night of November 14, 500 people were killed and 900 seriously injured.

—In Sheffield, 660 were killed in four days in December.

—In Liverpool, between December 1940 and May 1941, 2,400 people were killed

An eyewitness said, "I saw a trainload of troops pull into Waterloo Station just as a group of chattering children were boarding a train, evacuating them from London. Some of the men tried to hide their tears. They were just back from Belgium where they'd seen all the maimed and dead children during the Blitzkrieg. The tears were sheer relief at seeing kiddies escaping the horrors that were to come."

Unquestionably, when the *Volendam* and the *City of Benares* sailed, it was at the lowest point in the Battle of the Atlantic, and convoys set off inadequately guarded. Nevertheless, CORB decided that the benefits outweighed the risk, and they might well have been backed by parents under heavy air attack. In addition, the British public had total faith in the Royal Navy, the largest and most powerful navy in the world.

The CORB ships that joined large convoys of troopships were more fortunate. Three liners, the *Antonia, Duchess of York,* and *Oransay,* carrying a total of 1,131 CORB children to Canada, traveled in a convoy of troopships and enjoyed an escort of six destroyers and a battleship.

Similarly, a CORB ship, the *Batory,* heading for South Africa with a convoy of troopships heading to the Far East, was guarded by eight destroyers and three cruisers.

CORB was formed in response to an unprecedented outpouring of generosity on the part of Commonwealth countries. With invasion imminent, it was organized swiftly and efficiently and by including many organizations in the planning stages avoided a million pitfalls. During its brief life, it whisked many children to safety.

Parents ultimately made the decision regarding the risks. I do not envy my poor parents having to decide. For my father, having witnessed in WWI the atrocities perpetrated by invading armies, the decision would have been easier. He had two very pretty teenage daughters. I certainly feel for my poor mother, but unfortunately, never until now that it is too late.

Chapter Sixteen

*P*arents sending their children to safety under the CORB scheme believed it would be for just a year, or two at most. Few people imagined the war would last so long. During the five long years of war, the children changed, and parents had missed these gradual changes. After waving goodbye to a sweet little twelve-year-old girl, greeting a feisty seventeen-year-old young lady was quite a shock—as was the return of the five-year-old "baby" of the family as a gangly ten-year-old boy.

Some children received a jolt when they were told they were "going home." Home to a child who had left England at the age of five was the place they had been living in since 1940. They loved their foster parents and hated the thought of leaving them. Their own parents were unknown strangers.

For example, a bewildered, ten-year-old, Peter, gaped when his "mom" told him he would be going home in a week or two. Beaming, she acted as if she would be taking him to the ice hockey final. "But this is home," he insisted. "I don't want to leave."

"Of course, you do, dear. You're going home to your mummy and dad. That will be wonderful."

Confused, his eyes filling with tears, he ran to his bedroom. Scruffy, the family dog, followed and he sat on the floor hugging the dog. What was she talking about? Why did she want to get rid of him? His best friend lived next door, and he was going to be in the school concert.

Five years before, he had disembarked in Halifax and looked around eagerly for his mother. He had enjoyed the voyage and looked forward to telling his parents all about his "holiday." When his sister and an escort told him he was going to a foster family, he sobbed uncontrollably and arrived at his new home confused and frightened. He cried for an hour, and when his foster mother tucked him up in bed, he hid under the covers and wet the bed in the night. Something he had not done for several years. The understanding foster mother, pre-warned by the CORB organizers that some bed-wetting might occur with the youngest children, did not censure him, and gradually by kindness, won him over.

She enrolled him in a small nursery school, where he made friends with the neighborhood children, and gave him a puppy for Christmas. He settled down quickly and was soon calling her "mommy."

His ten-year-old sister, Pat, missed her parents and friends in England desperately. She had not wanted to leave. The war was fun. All sorts of exciting things were happening, and she would not be there. Her parents, well aware of the bombing to come, persuaded her to go along to take care of her brother.

After a bumpy few weeks, she started to enjoy school and made many friends. She still missed her parents, but memories faded and school activities soon engrossed her. When she heard they were going home, she was ecstatic. She longed to see her parents and all her old haunts.

Pat followed Peter to his room ten minutes later and found him on the floor, his face buried in Scruffy's fur. Putting her arm around him, she asked why he didn't want to go home. "You will be seeing all your friends in England and mum and dad. You'll love it."

Peter swallowed his sobs. "Why do mom and dad want to get rid of me? Have I been bad?"

"No, of course not. They don't want to get rid of you. It is just time for us to go home to our mum and dad."

"But, but . . . ," he hiccupped. "I don't remember who my mom and dad are, and anyway, they won't recognize me. Can't I just stay here with you and Scruffy?"

"No, we have to go. I'm looking forward to seeing home again and all our friends."

"But all my friends live here. I don't want to go."

His poor foster mother, who was upset at losing him, tried to reassure him, but until the day of his departure, he did not want to go to this strange country. However, he loved his sister, and she was going so reluctantly, he returned home. Once there, cuddled by an ecstatic mother and going to a bedroom full of his old toys, memories began to return. With the incredible resilience of a ten-year-old, he settled down once again.

Most were delighted to see their parents and relatives but found settling down far more difficult than in the host country. They had adapted to a different way of life. They had Canadian, Australian,

South African, and New Zealand accents, had spent five years in another school system, and wore clothes very different from their English counterparts. Having endured five years of clothes rationing, most British people wore gray drab clothes. These colorful creatures returning from other countries looked like peacocks in a flock of sparrows.

In the Dominions, teachers, foster parents, and other children had made allowances for them and helped them make the transition. It had been an exciting and challenging new life. Coming back to Britain was a different story. Other children mocked their "phony accents" and stories of another country which was so superior.

The contrast between sunny Northern Australia and gray, cold Northern England with bombed out buildings and food rationing would have been stark. Anthony, returning from an Australian summer to a gray Newcastle, remembers being staggered by the rows of flattened houses on Tyneside and the gaping ruins across the city.

Some boys, who had been evacuated at the age of fourteen or fifteen, had returned home earlier. Feeling guilty about escaping the war, they wanted "to do their bit," and on turning eighteen, volunteered for the British forces and were shipped home immediately.

A few boys who, at the age of sixteen, had joined the New Zealand Young Farmers' Program, which gave an agricultural education, guaranteed a place on a farm and the prospect of owning one, stayed on in New Zealand.

Having endured all the hardships of war and the separation from their children, parents were wildly excited to see them again. However, after the first few days of relatives rushing around to visit and welcome home parties, reality set in. These teenagers from a land of plenty complained constantly about the dreary diet.

They complained also about their clothes because again they wanted to fit in. With clothes rationing in place, the parents had to buy school uniforms, which left them short of coupons for out-of-school activities clothes. Teenagers were not adept at disguising their feelings as they surveyed their meager wardrobe.

However, for every child who had difficulties, another ten were delighted to be home with their parents again " . . . where they really belonged. Where it was their country, and they weren't constantly reminded of their 'different' background."

After a few weeks, all of them settled down in their old homes. They had enjoyed their experiences and returned far more broad-minded than their counterparts on either side of the Atlantic or Pacific.

Chapter Seventeen

*W*hen the *Volendam* sailed in 1940, the advantage lay with the U-boats. However, as the war progressed, the tide turned. Intelligence and anti-submarine weaponry improved. An additional fifty destroyers supplied by the U.S. meant convoys had more escorts and were no longer easy prey. The destroyers were supplied in exchange for ninety-nine-year leases on naval bases in Newfoundland, Bermuda, the Bahamas, Jamaica, St. Lucia, Trinidad, Antigua, and British Guiana.

The Battle of the Atlantic was long and bitter. In the beginning, U-boat captains observed the rules of the sea and helped survivors. Many surfaced and provided survivors with extra food and water and gave them a compass bearing to the nearest land. One captain saw a lone survivor on a raft with his shirt tied to an oar as a distress signal. He noted the bearing and continued on his mission to attack a convoy. After sinking two ships, he returned, and picked up the survivor. He had him wrapped in blankets, given a hot drink, and put in a bunk to thaw out. The captain then located a lifeboat of survivors and put the man on board with food, water, and a compass.

However, as U-boat losses mounted, Doenitz, unable to obtain replacements fast enough, instructed U-boat commanders to ignore survivors. On the surface, U-boats were vulnerable to both destroyer and aerial attack.

U-boat crews were feted heroes on land, but their losses were appalling. More than 713 U-boats were sunk, and 28,000 submariners died out of a total of 40,000. By 1945, the life expectancy of the average U-boat submariner was two missions. Of the 43,526 ships that sailed during the war, only 272 were sunk by U-boats.

Doenitz, commander of the U-boat flotillas of the Kriegsmarine, was an inspirational leader, and U-boat captains were flamboyant and daring. Many of their raids succeeded, but one adventurous captain failed. Under cover of darkness, he breached the U-boat barrier that guarded England's premier naval port of Portsmouth. Following close in the wake of a ship returning to port, he slipped deep into the harbor. Salivating at the thought of the lines of warships at anchor, he waited for the opportune moment to strike. However, while he waited, the tide ebbed.

A gray dawn disclosed a submarine high and dry on a mud bank. The embarrassed commander and crew stood with their hands in the air. The abandoned U-boat remained on the mud bank for the duration of the war. A constant delight to the people of Portsmouth who had suffered through endless Luftwaffe attacks.

Schnee, captain of the U-boat that torpedoed the *Volendam*, became one of the most successful submariners in the Battle of the Atlantic. His methodology was superb, and his successes earned him numerous decorations. He went on to become aide to Doenitz, and as Staff Officer Operations, Schnee helped plan the U-boat strategy that included hunting in wolf packs. A strategy that wreaked havoc on shipping as far afield as the U.S. East Coast. A good-looking man, he married Doenitz's daughter.

Schnee left, Doenitz center

Schnee survived the war and died in 1982 at the age of sixty-nine. He is remembered by officers of the British Navy when as Korvetan Kapitan he was present at the surrender of the U-boat fleet in Norway. An eyewitness said that Schnee, autocratic to the last, on seeing the British seamen with guns at the ready supervising the surrender, told them guns were not necessary. He said, "My men are disciplined. We have been told by Berlin to surrender, and we will carry out our orders. This will be a well-organized operation, and we would not like it marred by any shooting."

Now, decades later, as firm allies, submariners from Germany and England occasionally attend each other's reunions. Captain Mervyn Wingfield of the Royal Navy said Schnee was an impressive figure with whom he became quite friendly. He said, "Schnee had many decorations won for sinking a large tonnage of Allied shipping." He added, "Schnee told me, with a charming lack of modesty, 'Many other commanders received high decorations in the early part of the war when any fool could knock up a good score, but I won all my medals in 1941 and 1942 when things were pretty difficult for us.'" Schnee received two Iron Crosses, a Knights Cross in 1941, and a Knights Cross with Oak Leaves in 1942. On display in the British Submarine Museum in Gosport, England is a Kriegsmarine plaque presented by Schnee.

Allied merchantmen too paid a significant price; twenty-five percent of the men serving in the British Merchant Marine died in the North Atlantic. Their courage was phenomenal. Relatively defenseless in the face of U-boat and aerial attacks, they continued to sail time after time. Given the opportunity, stricken merchant ships rammed surfaced U-boats. Individual seamen too showed remarkable courage. Often dragged from the sea covered in oil after being torpedoed, they still signed on for another ship as soon as they reached port.

*   *   *

In the eighties, the British media organized a meeting between the teenage girl who had survived the sinking of the *City of Benares* and a seaman from U-48, the U-boat that torpedoed the ship. The girl had survived the disaster by swimming to an overturned lifeboat and hanging on to the keel until another lifeboat picked her up.

Later in the war, the seaman was captured and imprisoned in England. After his release, he stayed in England and became a builder. As elderly retirees, the two met and discussed the event. When the survivor of the City of Benares was asked by an interviewer whether she felt any animosity to the seaman, she replied, "Good heavens, no. He is a very nice gentleman, and he had no idea children were on board the ship."

*   *   *

Occasionally, good things come out of war. The fish benefited from the war at sea. With vessels under attack from air and sea, few trawlers ventured far out into the Atlantic. Thus, in spite of oil spills from sinking vessels, the fish stocks thrived and by the end of the war were far more numerous than at the beginning.

Chapter Eighteen

*L*ife in England changed dramatically when the war ended. After the wild delirium of the victory celebrations, the men returned home from battlefields across the world, and women gave up their jobs in factories and on the land. Our school had an influx of new, young teachers, and some of the older teachers who had stayed on through the war were able to retire. Industry faced the daunting task of rebuilding factories and docks, and the government surveyed the monumental national debt. Gold reserves had been emptied, and territories given away to fund two devastating wars.

A desire for change swept the country. People were tired of war, tired of inequality, and tired of sending their young men across the world to defend the Empire.

The election of 1945 proved to be a political sensation. A mere twelve weeks after the Nazis were defeated, Churchill was swept out of office by the Labor Party, a party that promised change.

True to its campaign promises, the new government introduced an overwhelming number of changes. The welfare state was born, offering a system of social insurance to every citizen regardless of income. This included a National Health Service that provided free medical treatment. The government nationalized industries, and the Empire, a constant drain on the armed forces, was replaced by the Commonwealth of Nations.

In 1946, the British Commonwealth of Nations, founded in 1931, became the Commonwealth of Nations consisting of former British colonies and Dominions that are all autonomous communities, independent of, and equal to Britain.

Today, one-third of the world's population lives within the Commonwealth, and Commonwealth countries constitute twenty-one percent of the world's land mass.

After the war ended, independence was granted to India, Pakistan, Burma (Myanmar), and Ceylon (Sri Lanka). India, Pakistan, and Sri Lanka opted to stay within the Commonwealth.

The Commonwealth has fifty four member countries. Of the fifty four, thirty three are republics, five have their own monarchs, and sixteen are a constitutional monarchy with the Queen of England as head of state. The Queen is also titular head of the Commonwealth.

Canada, Australia, and New Zealand are constitutional monarchies. South Africa opted out of the Commonwealth in 1961 due to the censure of other members for its policy of apartheid but was welcomed back in 1994 as the Republic of South Africa.

A Secretary-General is elected by the heads of government of the membership, and the Commonwealth Secretariat is headquartered in London. The heads of state gather every two years to discuss world and Commonwealth issues and agree to collective policies and initiatives.

Every four years, the Commonwealth gathers for the immensely popular Commonwealth Games. These are fiercely competitive but known as "The Friendly Games" because of the atmosphere in which they are held. I went to the 1990 Games in New Zealand and found this to be very true. The friendliness of the spectators, from all corners of the globe, made it a delightful experience. For example, two young men from the Falkland Islands competed in the 5,000 meters event. They ran with determination but were hopelessly outclassed by Kenyan, Australian, New Zealand, and British competitors. As the race progressed, they were left farther and farther behind but full of determination, they struggled on. Even though it was the last event of the day, everyone in the crowd remained in their seat. When they reached the bell lap, long after the rest of the field, all the crowd cheered and when they finally made it to the tape, they received a louder ovation than the winner.

*   *   *

Although Churchill's conservative government had lost the 1945 election, the country was never to forget the debt it owed him for his inspirational wartime leadership. A leadership that awoke the world to the perils of a dictator with overwhelming ambition and diabolical aims.

When Churchill died in 1965 at the age of ninety, he was given a State funeral. The only commoner to be accorded this honor in the twentieth century. His funeral was attended by kings, queens, presidents, and dignitaries from over one hundred countries.

The mourning was not confined to dignitaries. During the three days that his body lay in state at Westminster Hall in London, 320,000 people lined up three or four hours for the privilege of paying their respects. When his body was moved by gun carriage to St. Paul's Cathedral, people lined the route, five deep, in total silence.

His son, Randolph, said he held up well during the whole emotional service but was completely undone on the way to the family burial plot in Bladon, near Woodstock, Oxfordshire. As the train carrying the coffin traveled from London to its final destination, people lined the entire route, at every station, railroad crossing, and even fields, with heads bowed. Veterans in wheelchairs saluted.

The man who had inspired the country throughout the war was honored and never forgotten.

* * *

The overseas evacuation of children was cancelled after the threat of invasion disappeared. The children from the *Volendam* went back to their normal routine after their return home. Few of us believed the adventure had affected us, but it probably did in many ways. Certainly, a number of the boys, inspired by the bravery of the merchant navy, sought careers there after they graduated from high school.

The experience of meeting so many other young people from different parts of Great Britain and the *Volendam* crew from Holland broadened our view of life. We grew up eager to discover new places. In some, a sense of an unfinished journey lingered. As Jill Brown, my six-year-old friend said recently, "I felt I had been short changed by not reaching Canada." She rectified this by moving to Canada when she grew up. Getting married there, Mrs. Jill Mason continues to live happily with her family in Ontario.

Other children too migrated to the Dominions. With Australia and New Zealand offering assisted passages to British citizens, it was an attractive proposition. Several weeks on a luxury liner, a life in a new and exciting country in exchange for the princely sum of £10, and agreeing to remain in the country for two years. Anyone wishing to leave before this time paid their own way home.

Memories of our adventure faded. My siblings moved away from the Isle of Wight to further their education or pursue their careers. One by one, we left home. Basil went to the Merchant Navy College and graduated as a Navigation Officer, Margaret went into the WRNS, and Hazel to a bank in Brighton.

In 1955, Margaret and I embarked on another luxury liner bound for Canada. This time, the voyage was pleasant across benign seas. However, one day a thick fog enveloped the ship, and the temperature dropped dramatically as we neared an iceberg. As the doors to the watertight compartments clanged to a close, I felt the same claustrophobic chill run down my spine as I had on the *Volendam.*

We toured Canada from coast to coast for a year, working whenever we ran out of money, and visited relatives and several women from the village who had married Canadian soldiers.

At the end of the year, we returned home, and I was married a few months later. My husband and I left England in 1960 and spent time in Bermuda and several years in New Zealand where our son was born. Finally, we moved to California and enjoyed exciting careers in Silicon Valley as the computer industry grew at a frenetic pace. Retiring in our fifties, we spent fourteen years without a winter, moving between our homes in New Zealand, England, and California.

During this time, I was contacted by John Roberts, another survivor. He told me about the second torpedo that did not explode, and I realized for the first time that I had been leading a charmed life for decades.

Had the second torpedo exploded, the ship would have sunk within minutes, and few of us would have survived.

If a child in our group had not become sick when we returned to Scotland, we would have re-embarked on the ill-fated *City of Benares*.

To escape death so narrowly twice is a humbling experience.

However, it was a wonderful adventure, and the dangers were totally outweighed by the fun of meeting so many other young children.

Survivors of the *Volendam* to this day still hold meetings on August 30 to commemorate the event. The message with the sprigs of heather are still carefully kept in their treasured possessions along with the toys we were given. A brief episode in our young lives left an indelible impression.

Now my husband and I live close to my son and his family beside a lake in the beautiful Pacific Northwest. We spend many happy hours floating around on the pristine lake. However, before embarking on our boat, I always check for periscopes.

THE END

Glossary

ASDIC—anti-submarine detection device that uses sound propagation to detect the presence of submarines

ATS—Auxiliary Territorial Service. Women's army

Crocodile—a line of school children walking in pairs

Kriegsmarine—German Navy

Lascar—term for seaman of Indian or Indonesian nationality employed by the East India Company. Later, it became the common name for Indian seamen

Ludo—a board game in which counters are moved around in accordance with a throw of the dice.

Luftwaffe—German Air Force

Plimsoll—tennis shoe

RAF—Royal Air Force

RCMP—Royal Canadian Mounted Police

RNR—Royal Navy Reserve

U-BOAT—abbreviation for Unterseeboot (undersea boat) capable of operating under water. A submarine

WAAF—Women's Auxiliary Air Force

WLA—Women's Land Army. Women who worked on the land.

Wren—Sir Christopher Wren (1632-1723), one of Britain's most highly acclaimed architects. Designed St. Paul's Cathedral, London churches, Hampton Court, Kensington Palace, and the library at Trinity College Cambridge

WRNS—Women's Royal Naval Service

WVS—Women's Voluntary Service. Women who carried out voluntary services to help the war effort.

CHILDREN FROM THE ISLE OF WIGHT
ON BOARD *SS VOLENDAM*

Derek Brown
Jacqueline Brown (Mrs. Brooks)
Wendy (Jill) Brown (Mrs. Mason)
Valerie Butcher
Basil Cole
Hazel Cole
Ilene Cole (Mrs. Birkwood)
Margaret Cole (Mrs. Hocking)
Naomi Guy
Cecil Hayden
Pat Howe
John Roberts

*If any other of the above ladies are married, please accept my apologies.
This was the only information I could glean.*

Back row: Hazel Cole, Pat Howe, Jacqueline Brown, Margaret Cole, Valerie Butcher
Front row: Wendy (Jill) Brown, Ilene Cole, Naomi Guy